CANADA IN
2020

CANADA IN
2020

TWENTY LEADING VOICES
IMAGINE CANADA'S FUTURE

EDITED BY
RUDYARD GRIFFITHS

KEY PORTER BOOKS

Library and Archives Canada Cataloguing in Publication

Canada in 2020 : twenty leading voices imagine Canada's future / Rudyard Griffiths, editor.

Essays originally published in an editorial series in *La Presse* and the *Toronto Star*.

ISBN 978-1-55470-065-3

1. Canada—Forecasting. 2. Canada—History—21st century.
I. Griffiths, Rudyard

FC97.C34 2008   971.07   C2007-907333-6

ONTARIO ARTS COUNCIL
CONSEIL DES ARTS DE L'ONTARIO

The publisher gratefully acknowledges the support of the Canada Council for the Arts and
the Ontario Arts Council for its publishing program. We acknowledge the support of the
Government of Ontario through the Ontario Media Development Corporation's Ontario
Book Initiative.

We acknowledge the financial support of the Government of Canada through the Book
Publishing Industry Development Program (BPIDP) for our publishing activities.

Key Porter Books Limited
Six Adelaide Street East, Tenth Floor
Toronto, Ontario
Canada M5C 1H6

www.keyporter.com

Text design and formatting: Marijke Friesen

Printed and bound in Canada

08 09 10 11 12 5 4 3 2 1

CONTENTS

Acknowledgements   7

Introduction by Rudyard Griffiths   9

Imagining Canada's 153rd Birthday *by Andrew Cohen*   13

Canada under Attack: Story of a Foreseen Terror
   by Richard Hétu   21

São Paulo of the North: The Effects of Mass Immigration
   by Daniel Stoffman   29

The Baby Boomers' Tab: Already $40 Billion in 2020
   by Pierre Fortin   39

Whither the Canadian Economy? *by Don Drummond*   49

The United Nations in Decline *by Jennifer Welsh*   59

The Curse of Alberta *by Roger Gibbins*   67

Nalunaktuq: The Arctic as Force, Instead of Resource
   by Rachel A. Qitsualik   75

Two 2020 Scenarios *by George Elliott Clarke*   83

The Future of Democracy *by Mark Kingwell*   93

Canada sans Quebec: the Fifty-First State
   by Chantal Hébert   103

Boomers in an Ideological, Political, and Environmental
   Cauldron *by David Walker*   111

Ignoring the Canaries *by David Suzuki*   119

The Republic of Northern America *by Stéphane Kelly*   129

Canada's Economic Structure: Back to the Future?
   by Jim Stanford   139

A Fortunate Country *by David K. Foot*   149

Canadian Foreign Policy in 2020: A Different Player in a
    Different World *by Marie Bernard-Meunier*   159
Back to Work: Unemployment and the Fall and Rise of
    Canada's Traditional Values
    by Brian Lee Crowley   167
Canada and Its Peacekeepers in 2020 *by Noah Richler*   179
Since Time Immemorial (Plus Twelve Years)
    by Drew Hayden Taylor   191
Canada in 2020 *by Al Avlicino, citizen essay, winner*   199
A Canadian Unity Manifesto
    by Dave Hayward, citizen essay, runner up   203
Peace, Order, and Good Government: An Optimist's
    Opus *by Eric Mang, citizen essay, runner up*   209

Postscript by Rudyard Griffiths   213
About the Contributors   217

ACKNOWLEDGEMENTS

CANADA IN 2020 was launched on July 1, 2006, to spark a debate about the issues, events, and trends that could fundamentally transform Canada by the year 2020. The project originated with a series of articles in the *Toronto Star* and *La Presse* and a website (www.twenty-twenty.ca) where Canadians could write their own essays about what the country could look like in the year 2020 and join an online debate. Containing new essays by some of Canada's leading authors and the best citizen journalism as posted on our project website, this book marks the culmination of the Canada in 2020 project.

Canada in 2020 would not have been possible without a generous grant from The Aurea Foundation, a charitable organization founded in 2006 by industrialist Peter Munk and his wife, Melanie, to support institutions involved in the study and development of public policy. We want to acknowledge especially the help and guidance of Giles Gherson and Bob Hepburn of the *Toronto Star* and André Pratte at *La Presse*, who provided Canada in 2020 with a public voice and fuelled a meaningful national debate. The Dominion Institute would also like to extend our gratitude to Patricia Kennedy and Alison Faulknor, who tirelessly coordinated the efforts of our twenty authors, and Linda Pruessen of Key Porter Books, who was a driving force behind the project.

Finally, we would like to thank the authors, a passionate and dedicated group of thinkers, who were bold enough to take on this challenge and enlighten us with their vision of the country and the shape of things to come.

The Dominion Institute is a national charity founded in 1997 by a group of young people to promote greater knowledge of Canadian history and the informed discussion of public policy issues in Canada. For more information on the Dominion Institute, please visit www.dominion.ca.

INTRODUCTION

BY RUDYARD GRIFFITHS

EACH DAY 1.3 BILLION CHINESE wake up to confront a stark reality: China's blistering 10 per cent annual economic growth is increasingly underwritten by foreign energy supplies, primarily oil. In Iran, Africa, South America, and Canada's own oil sands, the Chinese are ruthlessly securing the energy supplies necessary to support an economy that is predicted to triple in size by the year 2020. Coping with the social upheaval caused by a roaring economy and ever mindful of its storied history of revolution, China's leadership knows that the future prosperity of the Middle Kingdom is inextricably linked with their ability to secure large amounts of natural resources, specifically oil and gas.

It's not just energy-starved giants such as China and the United States who are trying to figure out what policies and priorities they have to put in place today to preserve their way of life over the long term. On the other end of the geopolitical scale, the likes of Ireland, Singapore, and Finland are grappling with how to further the growth of their knowledge-based economies at a time when instant communication and new technologies allow developing nations to produce many of the same high-end products and services at a lower cost.

Through long-term investments in research, higher education,

9

and increased productivity, developed nations that have neither a superabundance of natural resources or large populations are discovering new ways to compete in the global marketplace and improve the quality of life of their citizens.

All of these countries—large and small, East and West, developed and developing—possess what is called a "strategic culture." Whether they face energy scarcity, regional instability, new technological paradigms, the threat of terrorism, or population growth, these nations grapple with immediate threats to their future welfare. These "externalities" create in a country, such as, say, Finland a strategic culture that allows its leadership to cut through red tape, sideline special interests, build consensus, and most important of all, forego short-term fixes to create policies that address long-term challenges.

Canada has been slow in developing its own strategic culture. For much of the twentieth century our geographic location and abundance of natural resources insulated us from the rest of the world. When major threats to our way of life did emerge we benefited from living beside the largest fire station in human history, whom we fought alongside in two world wars, the Korean War, and the Cold War.

In recent decades, two factors helped Canada create a homegrown strategic culture: a secessionist movement in Quebec and the challenge of sustaining a high standard of living with a small population in an era of globalization.

As debilitating as it seemed at the time, the threat of Quebec separation forced the country to confront its internal entropy and build the consensus necessary to patriate the Constitution (albeit imperfectly) and enshrine the Charter. Then, in the 1990s, in response to the pressures of globalization, Ottawa enacted painful but necessary long-term policies to reduce the federal debt and invest in education and research. Despite what was at times uninspired leadership and the near miss of the 1995 referendum, Canada benefited from having a series of well-defined national goals, such as unity, fiscal responsibility, and innovation.

Fast forward to today and our greatest challenge is increasingly the absence of any pressing issue(s) facing Canada. As the threat of Quebec separatism has receded and commodity prices have soared, no pressing impetus exists to help Canada renew its strategic culture and get about the work of allocating scarce human and material resources to pursue well-defined "national" goals or projects.

Find a way for Quebec to sign the *Constitution Act*? Confront the systemic failure of regional income assistance programs? Provide free post-secondary education to qualified high school graduates? Rationalize our immigration policies? Forget it. For a federal government awash in surpluses, it's easier to throw money at short-term fixes and sustain the status quo rather than build a stronger and more efficient federation. Case in point: only a quarter of government spending in recent federal budgets was on long-term investments (e.g., infrastructure, research, and post-secondary education)—some of the lowest ratios to total budget expenditures in the last two decades.

Without a strategic culture born of shared challenges and equipped to advance common national goals, Canada risks becoming a shadow of its former self, a collection of disparate regions, interests, and groups all bickering over the unearned spoils of a resource-based economy destined eventually to go bust.

Right now Canadians, unlike Chinese and Americans, and a host of other more powerful countries, have the material wealth and room to manoeuvre to renew a strategic vision for the country's future. Do we, for instance, want to be known as the first G8 nation to have a "green" economy? Should we extend our efforts in Afghanistan and become the world's leaders in rebuilding failed states? Or is it time to finally get serious about using our present-day prosperity to build a knowledge-based economy for the time when commodity prices go into a tailspin?

We need to anticipate now the issues that will shape our collective future, and set about developing national priorities and goals to manage the challenges that lie ahead. This is the raison d'être of our Canada in 2020 initiative and the motivation behind the publication of this book. By bringing our country's sharpest minds and brightest thinkers together to peer into the decade ahead, Canadians can begin to debate today what priorities we should be tackling to secure a bright and prosperous future. Hard-won experience of generations past tells us that to tarry too long in the safe and comfortable present is a luxury we cannot long afford.

IMAGINING CANADA'S 153ᴿᴰ BIRTHDAY

BY ANDREW COHEN

Oᴛᴛᴀᴡᴀ, Jᴜʟʏ 1, 2020—On the 153ʳᵈ anniversary of Confederation, Canada goes through the motions yet again. On Parliament Hill, the bells toll mournfully and the Maple Leaf hangs listlessly. Soldiers fire a twenty-one-gun salute and Snowbirds fly overhead. Under sweltering skies, the prime minister still insists that Canada is "a young country," as he and his untutored predecessors have done since it really was a young country.

Thousands gather on the grass. They hear breathless politicians declare that Canada is the best country in the world, a boast once thought terribly un-Canadian, but lately as predictable as the national time signal. In the shadow of the Peace Tower, they watch entertainers of every ethnicity reflecting this extraordinarily diverse society. The show is as inclusive as Canada itself. Everyone must be represented—there was a minor scandal last year when Karen dancers from Burma were overlooked in the festivities—because peoples from around the globe are reserving rooms in Hotel Canada. All want a role in this spectacle, as if to confirm their arrival.

Troupe after troupe of new Canadians in traditional national costume march across the stage. Recalling national birthdays long past, there are some high-stepping Ukrainians, fiddlers from Quebec, and throat singers from Nunavut. But these are passé today. Now the headliners are drummers from Senegal and acrobats from Brunei. After a half-generation of open immigration, Canada is home to millions who have fled the drought and desertification that have turned parts of Africa and Asia into a netherworld and made the environment humanity's ruin. The land that God gave to Cain and Voltaire called "a few acres of snow" now looks like Shangri-La in a warmer world. No wonder Canada's birthday party goes on for three days, as if it were a Hindu wedding.

This is the new complexion of Canada: black, tan, and yellow. Canadians are proud to call themselves the most moderate of people. Tolerance has become their vocation, a kind of raison d'être, and that seems to be the breadth of their ambition. In a fragmenting world spawning new countries as casually as Arctic glaciers crack and calve, they are happy to have survived as a nation for a century and a half—even if they're not sure what that means anymore.

No, this isn't your father's Canada. Nor is it the Canada of Sir John A. Macdonald, Mackenzie King, Lester Pearson, Brian Mulroney, Pierre Berton, Margaret Atwood, Michael Bliss, Douglas Coupland, or Avril Lavigne. They would not recognize it, and few in this new country would recognize them. The nation roams around under a cloud of amnesia, as if nothing happened before yesterday. This summer holiday—what do they call it? This capital—what does it represent? This Parliament—what does it do? July 1 was once Canada Day (in prehistoric times, it was Dominion Day) and this was a national celebration. Ottawa was a national capital and Parliament was a national legislature.

There is no "national" anymore because there is no nation, at least not as we knew it. In 2020, Canada is a country in little more than name. It has taken the nineteenth-century idea of the nation-state and turned it on its head; Canada is now a collection of many nations (its ethnic minorities) who know only their own past, and many states (its provinces) that now know only their own interests. For many who have come here, Canada is a country of convenience. It offers security and anonymity and asks for conformity and equanimity. People take rooms in this grand hotel, as novelist Yann Martel once put it, with little knowledge of—or attachment to—the place itself. In a rootless world of shifting loyalty and no fixed address, Canada is just another comfort station on the road to somewhere else. As author George Jonas once put it, Canada is a railway station in which passengers share "a destination but no destiny."

The federal government is an antique notion in the era of sub-governments and supra-governments. Canada's provinces have turned into princely states like those of British India, governed by pashas who have the powers of minor monarchs. Within these kingdoms are city states. "National," an anachronistic term, now competes with "provincial" and "municipal" at home and "international" abroad.

So, "Canada Day" is now called "People's Day," a celebration of our great mingling of races from the corners of the Earth. The Canadian Parliament is no longer a supreme body of lawmakers but a jumped-up town council of superannuated time-servers taking up space in that grand Gothic pile on the Ottawa River. The House of Commons has had little to do since the federal government transferred its remaining powers to the provinces some ten years ago. No wonder Ottawa is only a symbol of the government these days. It is overshadowed by the real centres of power in post-Confederation Canada—Vancouver, Edmonton, Toronto, and Montreal— that drew the country's best minds from Ottawa, as Pierre Elliott Trudeau had warned long ago. In happier times, a travel writer compared Ottawa to Cetinje, the capital of Montenegro up to 1918. Now, with cruel irony, it is Cetinje that has reclaimed its imperial glory as the seat of a renewed Montenegro, while Ottawa has become a backwater in a diminished Canada.

What we have here is a virtual country. In the five-hundred-nation universe, Canada is an area code and an email address. Yes, it is still fantastically rich, awash in petrodollars, endowed with mountains, forests, minerals, and unfathomable space between three great oceans. Its biggest export is water, and it is more expensive than oil. But today, 153 years after it was created, a visitor from the past might wonder what the country is celebrating. After all, what is Canada, anyway?

Physically, it may be hard to tell the difference between what the country was two decades ago and what it is in 2020. It will surprise many to learn that Canada still includes Quebec, despite all those bond traders and currency speculators who thought otherwise and lost money. With all of Quebec's new powers, the sovereignists shrewdly concluded that independence would be unnecessary, even redundant. After all, with federalism like this, who needs sovereignty?

But there is indeed a new Canada, and it is the product of twin forces that had been at work for some time. Contemporary historians have come to call them "the great migration" and "the quiet devolution."

The "great migration" was a byword for the greatest influx of immigrants Canada had ever known. By 2012, the country's political parties were treating immigration as an auction, bidding against each other for ethnic voters in urban Canada to raise the quotas of immigrants from 250,000 to 500,000 a year. There was a sound economic reason (a shortage of unskilled labour) and a moral reason (boatloads of refugees were washing up on our shores, just as they were in Spain, Malta, and Sicily). As global warming began to wreak havoc around 2014, a suddenly popular Green Party formed the government in Ottawa. The United Nations began to pressure empty, enormous Canada to ease the refugee crisis. By opening the country's borders, politicians could feel that they'd helped the world, as well as themselves.

Of course, immigration has benefited Canada. Even with a low birth rate the population grew from thirty-three million in 2008 to thirty-eight million in 2012 to forty-five million in 2018. Within two years, Statistics Canada predicts there will be fifty million Canadians. Fifty million! Finally, in size, Canada is the nation that Sir Wilfrid Laurier imagined a century ago.

While the influx has made the country's big cities even bigger (Toronto's population is now eleven million, served by high-speed rail service and three airports), it has developed regions like northern Ontario, where Sudbury, Sault St. Marie, Thunder Bay, and North Bay are flourishing. Down

East, immigrants have re-made Saint John, Moncton, and Halifax. They have also made things interesting. Oh, how things have changed in old, staid, Anglo-Saxon Canada. You can now eat pad Thai in Red Deer and chapatis in Estevan.

For the most part, Canada has taken a laissez-faire view to its new arrivals. Multiculturalism is a kind of narcissism for Canadians. We are in love with it and the image it gives us around the world. We look down at old Europe for its difficulty in integrating immigrants of different cultures, spawning ghettos in lily-white Stockholm, Amsterdam, and Oslo.

Still, as immigration has brought Canada prosperity, it has also brought it ambiguity. No one has taught these new Canadians much about their new country, its past, its triumphs, its myths. In Canada, where the provinces are responsible for education, no one teaches Canadian history anymore. Captured by the canons of political correctness, schools celebrate multiculturalism as an end in itself, failing to teach the superiority of civic nationalism over ethnic nationalism. No one speaks for Canada anymore; worse, no one speaks of Canada. No one knows what it was or is. East Indians, Pakistanis, and Chinese come here and live their lives happily in Hindi, Urdu, and Mandarin. Sadly, they import their prejudices and struggles, too, which often find violent expression in the country's grim urban corridors.

But as the country changed you couldn't talk about this. The public campaign to persuade immigrants to adopt our mores and accept our rules was attacked as chauvinistic, even racist. Over time we diminished our citizenship, offering it freely and asking little in return. We became more interested in rights than responsibilities. The truth was that few Canadians of the last generation shared very much with each other, and even fewer have known what it means to be Canadian. No one has told them. It begged a variation of the biblical question: What hath a country if it gaineth the world but loseth its soul? If Canada was becoming more cosmopolitan, it was also becoming less cohesive.

While the wave of immigrants was flooding across our borders, the provinces were re-asserting themselves. They demanded more powers—and they got them. This is the other part of the re-making of Canada. There was a time Confederation represented a division of powers between governments. Once the province of the province was the province; now the province of the province is the nation, for that is how they see themselves. The quiet devolution has created swaggering potentates presiding over wealthy fiefdoms, especially Alberta, which continually threatened to leave. This happened subtly, through administrative agreements, when no one was looking. It was the natural outcome of decades of whining and petitioning. True, it had been going on since the 1960s, but the system always assumed an intergovernmental negotiation, not unilateral disarmament.

In 2014, the centre collapsed. The provinces already had spending power, taxing power, and their own pensions and social programs. They were choosing their immigrants and even running their own foreign policies. Indeed, for more than a decade they had embassies—no one bothered with the fiction of calling them "tourist offices" or "cultural legations" anymore—in international capitals. When the government allowed Quebec to send a representative to UNESCO, the province soon asked the same for the World Health Organization, the Human Rights Council, and the International Labour Organization. As usual, what Quebec got, all provinces got. Now a once-influential country speaks to the world not with a single, eloquent voice, but in a contradictory and confusing cacophony.

When the provinces started raising their own armies—the last great federal preserve—the game was over. Ottawa handed the provinces monetary policy and divided up its military assets. The centre had nothing but the Royal Canadian Mint, the Canada Post, and the Parliament buildings, now a Victorian architectural curiosity for Chinese tourists.

All along, of course, the accommodationists said this was the price of unity. Quebec was still in, wasn't it? Alberta and Newfoundland, with their oil wealth, had not left us, had they? We had chanted the hymn of unity for so long that it had become a mantra, blinding us from seeing our purpose as a nation. In the name of unity, we abandoned the symbols of our nationhood, allowed the provinces a free hand in the world, stopped teaching history, shared no collective ideas, and promoted no great project beyond diversity itself. Oh, we were a good country, but not a great one.

Now, in 2020, we look around in despair. In the voiceless country, there is no one left to recall its past, no one left to celebrate its principles, and no one left to speak its name.

CANADA UNDER ATTACK: STORY OF A FORESEEN TERROR

BY RICHARD HÉTU

July 5, 2020

Since September 11, 2001, reliable sources have been repeating the warning: Canada, like any other industrialized Western country, is not sheltered from a wide-scale terrorist attack. And yet, for nearly twenty years we have been protected, day after day, by the grace of God, CSIS, or luck. Unfortunately, this state of affairs came to an end this afternoon in the Montreal metro.

What a contrast between the images of the planes smashing into the Twin Towers of the World Trade Center and those from July 5, 2020! By the end of the evening, the Web had started broadcasting images of the attack caught on "smart video" by the public transit system; absolutely nothing explosive, just the cold determination to kill in large numbers, in my hometown.

The new cameras in the Montreal metro didn't miss a thing, or almost. Installed after the Boston subway attacks, they scan every centimetre of the system—waiting areas, trains, tunnels, and platforms—producing video images that are immediately transformed into digital data. This surveillance system, fruit of Québécois innovation, can detect, categorize, and follow objects or people of interest according to user-defined specifications. In principle, it can receive real-time alerts and react proactively to threats. It is the very pinnacle of technology.

But will the video of the attack one day be shown on Canadian television? Tonight, broadcasters completely censored it, bending to the requests of authorities, who have promised to find and punish the person or people responsible for a leak that allowed a small-time blogger in Vermont, in the United States, to stream images of the attack over the Internet. These made their way around the globe in seconds. On their websites, Canadian news sources were forced to be content to tell the story in words and photos. Here are the facts, unendurable though they are:

Between 5:19 p.m. and 5:24 p.m., at the peak of the evening rush, five individuals wearing baseball caps get up from their seats in five different trains all heading for Berri station, the busiest in the metro system. From a gym bag, each of them pulls out a portable spray gun, similar to the Canadian Model 5 tear-gas ejector. Then, turning around slowly, they spray a fast-acting nerve agent into the air of each of the five cars.

The passengers do not know that the dangerous gas, tabun, can kill by inhalation or contact with skin within twenty minutes. It doesn't take them long, though, to realize they are the victims of a chemical or biological attack. How long this kind of threat has been talked about! In the packed trains, the cameras record panic spreading from face to face. However, these same cameras are unable to make out the features of the faces hidden under the terrorists' caps.

In each of the besieged trains, it is a matter of some ten seconds between the start of the attack and the opening of the doors. The passengers' first move is not to subdue the terrorists but to flee the gas-filled cars. The commandos follow them, gassing an increasing number of passengers in their wake.

It is roughly another ten seconds between the doors opening and the terrorists being gunned down by police. Thanks to the smart video, the alert to the attack was set off the moment the terrorists brandished their spray guns. Nevertheless, over the course of the twenty to twenty-five seconds that followed, hundreds of passengers would have inhaled the fruit-scented gas that paralyzes the respiratory system and causes the lungs to constrict.

In the wee hours of the morning, the number of victims is unknown and no one has yet taken credit for the attacks. One thing is certain, according to commentators, who can't avoid the circumstantial cliché: Canada will never be the same. Knowing what happened to the United States after the attacks of September 11, this is not particularly reassuring.

July 6, 2020

No one could accuse the Canadian authorities—municipal, provincial, or federal—of not having taken the threat of chemical or biological terrorism seriously. After the VX Boston subway attack that left 197 dead and 461 wounded, they poured every effort into attack prevention and disaster management.

Thus, the different levels of government agreed on a specific strategy in the event of an attack—the Equinox Plan—which was put into effect yesterday. The necessary hospital staff was mobilized to deal with the victims at specific facilities in seven major Montreal hospitals, as designated by the federal and provincial health ministries.

Alerted at the same time as police, paramedics, fire-fighters, and other emergency personnel, all wearing protective suits, arrived at Berri station shortly after the terrorists were gunned down. Thanks to their individual dosimeters, ambulance staff identified the type of gas used in the attack and recognized with consternation that there was nothing they could do for the majority of the victims. Tabun, a gas created in 1936 and used by Iraq during the Iran-Iraq War, belongs to a group of toxic and infectious agents for which Canada no longer has a vaccine or antidote, says a Montreal newspaper, citing anonymous sources within the federal government. At a time when threats seem to evolve with the seasons—and biotechnological progress—Montreal hospitals do not deal with it anymore.

Did the terrorists know? Conspiracy theorists were not the only ones to wonder this upon hearing the first count of the victims: 310 dead and only 15 wounded, a tally that attests to the superior quality of the gas. As in many Western countries, including the United States, France, and the United Kingdom, the quantity and makeup of antidote, antibiotic, and vaccine stocks are government secrets in Canada. The vaccines or antidotes to which the government has access—or, more to the point, the vaccines or antidotes to which it does not have access in sufficient quantities, if at all—is information that terrorist networks would be eager to put to use.

This raises the question on many people's minds: Could there be a traitor or traitors among us?

If there is paranoia, it is but one of the manifestations of the shock felt today from one end of Canada to the other. Sorrow, sympathy, patriotism, and anger are also in the mix. On television and radio, in the newspapers and on the Internet, politicians, experts, and citizens have expounded on the hateful and insidious nature of the attack.

"Despite advances in genetic invention, gas is still probably the most powerful and effective instrument of terror available," stated an expert. Another opined: "The possession of these weapons gives terrorists the opportunity to blackmail the governments of small and large countries, to sow the seeds of hate and panic in the population in general." Yet another asked, "Why on Earth does Canada not have an antidote to tabun anymore? Of all the neurotoxic agents, isn't it the easiest to make?"

In Ottawa and Quebec, Opposition parties have demanded public inquiries into the makeup of strategic stocks of strategic health products. The issue is not only crucial in the event of a chemical or biological attack, but also to deal with the possibility of a pandemic.

While Montreal and Quebec authorities wait for these inquiries to be carried out, they have attempted to reassure metro users by promising to introduce new "protective" measures. In particular, they have announced the installation of sophisticated detectors that can recognize weapons, plastic explosives, and chemical, biological, and radioactive products. Each subway turnstile should soon be monitored by one of these detectors. Employed in many North American subways—in New York, Boston, Chicago, and Toronto, among others—the system should cause no slowdown of service, unless there is an alert.

The technology was available as of 2014, but it would require an attack before it made its appearance in the Montreal metro.

As for the cameras, they will continue to scan everything in their path, and not only the activities of potential criminals or terrorists. Ten years after their installation, it is rare that people raise concerns of privacy.

We live in a time where safety comes first.

July 7, 2020

We've been saying it non-stop since the attack: On July 5, 2020, the Canadian psyche received a devastating shock; its population, long accustomed to peace, now finds itself at war with an unknown enemy. Not only does responsibility for the attack go unclaimed, but also authorities, scorning the media's repeated requests, refuse to release any information on the terrorists killed in the subway.

Canadians of all types have certainly pointed the finger at radical Islamists, whether they've immigrated here or grown up among us. Neo-Nazi groups have gone further by burning down mosques in Montreal, Toronto, and Calgary, among other cities. Still today, authorities call for calm. Still today, the media shows restraint. Yet the coincidence is remarkable: The attack in the Montreal metro occurred one week after

Canada's official refusal to recognize the new Islamic republic born out of the revolution in Saudi Arabia. In so doing, Ottawa followed in Washington's footsteps, where the Republican administration is ready for action.

The Canadian psyche most definitely did receive a shock, but certain reflexes remain. Yesterday, a Toronto columnist wrote that the tabun attack drove a final nail in the coffin of the Quebec separatist movement.

"The separatists want to create a country where the army would be abolished and replaced with a peace force. There is no more peace, not even in Quebec," he wrote.

It was to be expected. This morning, the Republic of Quebec commentators—the francophone ones, to be more accurate—reacted to this comment with irritation, indeed, indignation. Separatist or federalist, Quebec commentators were united in their condemnation of the Toronto journalist's lack of tact.

"If the tabun attack calls an ideology into question, it isn't Quebec separatism, but rather Canadian multiculturalism," wrote one Montreal columnist, having already attributed the attack to radical Islam. "This ideology should have died the day Ontario renounced plans to institute sharia law for family litigation. Alas, it still continues to serve as an argument for our fundamentalists."

July 8, 2020
After the shock and the mourning, here is the surprise. The tabun attack wasn't linked to September 11, 2001, as we had thought, but rather to March 20, 1995. Its perpetrators are

presumed to be part of a religious organization more closely resembling the Aum Shinrikyo sect, responsible for the sarin attack in the Tokyo subway, than al Qaeda, sponsor of the World Trade Center and Pentagon attacks.

The Canadian prime minister dropped this bomb this morning, at the same time announcing the arrest of the leaders of the Canadian sect, named Supreme Victory, whose headquarters are located in the Eastern Townships in Quebec. Known for its apocalyptic prophecies, the organization has small offshoots in all Canadian provinces as well as in several U.S. states. Like the suicide bombers, its disciples are representative of the ethnic diversity of North America. During the sect's last public declaration, less than a year ago, its leader, known as Victor I, predicted a series of spectacular events signalling the end of civilization. As usual, no one took it seriously.

SÃO PAULO OF THE NORTH: THE EFFECTS OF MASS IMMIGRATION

BY DANIEL STOFFMAN

IT'S 2020 AND, IN TORONTO, the days when everyone used the public health-care system are gone. So is the time when a majority of affluent, middle-class parents sent their kids to public schools. In 2020, vast tracts of suburban slums occupy what used to be good farmland on the city's outskirts. Traffic congestion and air pollution are unbearable. Toronto's reputation as one of North America's most liveable cities is a distant memory. It's now known as the "the São Paulo of the north."

This dystopian vision of the future of Canada's largest city is hardly far-fetched. Toronto is already suffering severe growing pains, the result of the federal government's insistence on maintaining the world's largest per capita annual immigration intake—around 250,000 people a year of whom about 40 per cent come to Toronto. That's around 100,000 newcomers year after year after year. It is impossible for any city to maintain its social and physical infrastructure in the face of such relentless population growth. By 2020, Greater Toronto's population will have ballooned from five million to seven million—or even more if immigration levels are raised higher still.

Every year Mercer Human Resource Consulting ranks world cities according to their liveability. Vancouver always places at or near the top of the list while the other big Canadian cities are among the top thirty. Most of the top-ranked cities are relatively small—places like Copenhagen (500,000) and Zurich (340,000). None of the world's vast urban agglomerations of ten million or more, such as São Paulo and Seoul, are rated by Mercer as desirable places to live. Smaller big cities are more liveable because their residents can enjoy the amenities of urban life without the congestion, crime, and pollution associated with sprawling megalopolises.

Canada's liveable cities are an unsung national asset. One of the things that makes them special is the presence of immigrants from all over the world, who have contributed new energy and cultural diversity. But, in immigration as in everything else, too much of a good thing isn't better. Ottawa's policy of mass immigration, for which no reasonable explanation has ever been offered, risks doing irreparable damage to our cities.

This policy of rapid urban growth is being implemented by Ottawa even though it has no jurisdiction over urban affairs and even though the policy has never been stated explicitly. Yet the impact is already evident. Highway 401 across Toronto has become the most congested road in North America, waste disposal is an intractable problem, and the public schools can't afford to provide the English instruction newly arrived children need. In Vancouver, meanwhile, controversy raged over the British Columbia government's decision to twin the Port Mann Bridge that links the rapidly growing Fraser Valley suburbs to the city.

Amazingly, the local politicians who have to cope with the results never suggest that perhaps the immigration intake might be lowered from time to time, as was standard practice until the late 1980s. To listen to their silence, one would think the relentless influx of huge numbers of new residents was a natural phenomenon like the weather rather than a deliberate federal policy that could easily be changed.

Ottawa might claim it is not to blame for unmanageable urban growth because it just lets the immigrants in, it doesn't tell them where to go. But this would be disingenuous, because the federal government knows that Toronto gets 40 per cent of all immigrants while Vancouver gets 14 per cent, and Montreal 15 per cent. Many of those who settle elsewhere at first also eventually wind up in one of the three biggest cities. Attempts at dispersion are ineffective, because immigrants want to live where previous cohorts of the same ethnicity are already established. They also want to live in cities for the same reason Canadian-born people do—they are more likely to find jobs there.

The country most comparable to Canada is Australia. Like Canada, it is an English-speaking Commonwealth nation settled in relatively recent history. Like Canada, it has an organized immigration program and has used immigration effectively to enhance population growth and increase the vigour and diversity of its major cities. Australia's current net migration rate (immigration minus emigration per 1,000 of population) is 3.78. Canada's is 5.79. Before the Progressive Conservative government of Brian Mulroney increased immigration levels and made them permanent during the latter part of the 1980s, a policy continued by the Liberals under Jean Chrétien, Canada had an intake similar, on a per capita basis, to Australia's.

There is no reason why Canada should have more immigration than any other country. Canada's existing population is younger than those of most other developed countries and its ratio of working-age people to retired ones is higher. If Canada reverted to its traditional, more moderate, immigration program, it could continue to enjoy the benefits of immigration while sparing its cities the problems of unmanageable growth.

Immigrants would benefit too. Their economic performance has been in freefall over the past fifteen years. Previously the number of new immigrants varied according to labour market needs. Sometimes it would be cut to give the newly arrived a chance to be absorbed successfully into the economy without intense competition from more new arrivals. Not anymore. An endless stream of newcomers arrives in the big cities with few options but to work in poorly paid jobs such as cleaning houses and driving taxis. Wages of these jobs are thus kept low, and those who do them have little chance to get ahead.

Previously, poverty levels among immigrants were about the same as those of the Canadian-born. Now they are much worse. According to a report by the Canadian Council on Social Development, whereas the poverty level of those who arrived before 1986 was 19.7 per cent, or slightly lower than that of the Canadian-born, the poverty level of those who came after 1991 was an alarming 52.1 per cent, while that of people born in Canada remained unchanged at around 20 per cent.

If this trend is not reversed, the major cities will be home, by 2020, to an entrenched underclass living in slums. Because of gentrification and rising property values in the central cities, these slums will be located in the suburbs, requiring long commutes for those fortunate enough to have employment.

Toronto Star reader Fan Yang shrewdly analyzed the impact of federal immigration policy in a letter to the newspaper in 2003. He accused the federal government of "dumping more cheaply acquired labour into the domestic labour pool, regardless of whether there is a healthy demand. Businesses welcome that enthusiastically as they bear no direct cost of unemployed immigrants and only garner the rewards of lower labour costs."

Even skilled workers are doing poorly. According to the 2001 census, male immigrants with a university degree who came to Ontario in the late 1990s were earning, after six to ten years in Canada, only 54 per cent of that earned by native-born Canadians in that province with similar qualifications. Even the youngest, presumably most employable, immigrants are doing worse than in the pre-Mulroney era of moderate immigration levels. Employment in the twenty-five to forty-four age group fell from 75.7 per cent in 1981 to only 65.8 per cent in 2002. During the same period, employment of non-immigrants rose to 81.8 per cent from 74.6 per cent. "Sixty per cent of skilled immigrants who come here are unemployed or underemployed," Kevin McLellan, project manager of hireimmigrants.ca, an employment website, told the *Toronto Sun* in 2008.

Remarkably, immigrant labour-market performance has declined during a time of increasing shortages of skilled workers. But, as the above data suggest, just bringing in huge numbers of people doesn't solve skills shortages. Mexico has a worse skills shortage than Canada, yet it has no shortage of people. The trick is to match immigrants to jobs, and our current immigration program doesn't do that well. Luckily, Canada doesn't need to reinvent the wheel. It merely needs to emulate the solutions that Australia's more successful immigration program has already found, such as requiring the credentials of skilled immigrants to be approved before they come and imposing strict requirements for language skills.

In an attempt to improve the performance of immigrants and to better meet labour force needs, the federal government in March 2008 introduced amendments to its budget bill to allow the immigration minister to give preference to some applications. If, for example, there were a pressing need for skilled construction workers, such applicants could be given preference over others lacking the required skills.

The controversy that erupted over these amendments reflected a key issue. Who decides who gets into Canada: The government acting in the national interest or the immigrants themselves? Organizations claiming to speak for immigrants opposed the amendments because they want easy access to Canada for the extended families of existing immigrants, even though these family members may have none of the linguistic or occupational qualifications that would allow them to succeed in a modern industrial economy.

One of the most bizarre comments came from Dalton McGuinty, Ontario's premier, who opposed the amendments because, if barriers to unskilled immigrants had been in place, his family could not have emigrated from Ireland to Canada during the 1845–52 potato famine. In the *Toronto Star* (March

27, 2008), he said, "We had no skills, we couldn't speak English, and we were dirt poor. But we were looking for opportunity and we brought with us a solid work ethic."

McGuinty did not seem to understand that Canada in 1850 had good reason to welcome people who were prepared to clear bush for farms, build roads, and do many other labour-intensive tasks. It did not matter if these new arrivals were illiterate and unskilled. The young colony needed them as much, if not more, than it needed chemists, clerks, and librarians.

In 2008, there are no well-paying jobs for uneducated people who cannot speak English or French and have no specialized occupational training. Yet McGuinty wants to keep Canada's doors wide open to such people because his ancestors were also unskilled. In other words, the selection criteria for immigrants should be the same in 2008 as it was 150 years ago.

All other public policies change in accordance with changing conditions. Canada's economic, environmental, and transportation policies are not the same in 2008 as they were in 1850. It is difficult to understand why Ontario's premier thinks immigration policy must remain frozen in time.

In addition to creating poverty, mismanaged immigration is weakening our public health-care and education systems. By 2020, the huge baby-boomer cohort of Canadians will be entering its stage of heaviest reliance on the health-care system. The boomers will not tolerate interminable waits for hip replacements and cancer treatment. As if the challenge of caring for impatient boomers weren't enough, the presence of millions of new immigrants will intensify the demands on the system.

Many of the newcomers will be old, because Canada is the most generous country in allowing immigrants to sponsor elderly parents and grandparents.

There is no chance that our health-care system can survive in its current form given the increased demands on it from these demographic changes. As a result, by 2020 a full-fledged parallel private health-care system will be in operation in the major immigrant-receiving cities, which are also where most of the boomers live. Private health care will be relied upon not just by the wealthy but by much of the middle class as well. A similar transformation will occur in education. A report prepared in 2006 for the Elementary Teachers of Toronto said teachers were spending the equivalent of one day a week trying to make up for the lack of English-as-a-second-language support for their immigrant students. "The more time the regular classroom teacher is having to devote to ESL students . . . it detracts from the level of service we want for all of our students," union president Martin Long told the *Globe and Mail*.

In other words, the lack of support for ESL students is hurting all students. This is certainly not the fault of the immigrant children. It is the fault of rash and ill-conceived federal policy. As a result, by 2020 most middle-class families will have abandoned the public system. This will be an unfortunate development because the public schools are where immigrants and Canadian-born get to know each other. They are an important force for social cohesion.

One of the most common arguments for very high immigration levels is that "immigrants do the jobs Canadians won't do." In fact, Canadian-born people always have and still do the most dangerous and dirty jobs, such as mining and garbage collection. But they expect to be decently paid for their work. The "jobs Canadians won't do" argument is a euphemism for saying Canada should use immigration to compress wages— a sure formula for exacerbating urban poverty.

A seemingly plausible argument for boosting the population of at least one Canadian city to ten million or more would be that the truly great cities of the world are very large. But London and Paris grew to their current size gradually over hundreds of years, and their greatness is the result of the wealth of the empires of which they were the capitals. You don't build London and Paris by adding millions of bodies over a short period of time. That's how you build Mumbai and Mexico City.

In the *Ottawa Citizen* (November 2, 2005), Ontario's environment commissioner, Gord Miller, issued a warning about what the future holds for Toronto given current trends: "The environmental impacts of this magnitude of growth . . . will compromise the quality of our lifestyle to a stage where it will be unrecognizable," he said. "We already have trouble dealing with our waste right now. . . . What about another four million tonnes a year? What about another four million cars?"

The current federal government's first immigration minister, Monte Solberg, told a House of Commons committee that he was concerned about the "huge burden" high immigration levels place on our major cities. He thus became the first immigration minister in at least two decades to show any sensitivity to the impact of immigration policy on the urban environment.

Now it's the turn of local officials to abandon their ostrich-like refusal even to mention immigration when discussing urban growth. Perhaps they fear being branded "anti-immigrant" if they do. But Pierre Trudeau, in his last year as prime minister, cut immigration by 25 per cent, and no one called him anti-immigrant. In that case, good management trumped politics. It's an example the Conservative government would do well to follow.

THE BABY BOOMERS' TAB: ALREADY $40 BILLION IN 2020

BY PIERRE FORTIN

CANADIAN BABY BOOMERS are soon going to retire en masse, and they are going to leave fewer children behind. The annual cost: already $40 billion (in 2008 dollars) by 2020. Just after the Second World War, from 1945 to 1960, there were about 28 births on average per 1,000 people in Canada: These were the children of the baby boom. But these baby boomers did not have many children of their own, and it does not look like they are going to have many grandchildren either. By 1970, the birth rate in Canada had dropped to 17 births per 1,000 people. Since 2000, it has been hovering around 11 births per 1,000 Canadians.

This extraordinary flip-flop in the birth rate explains a number of key phenomena in our collective life during the last fifty years. It will now have a determining influence on the economic and social change that we will witness during the coming decades, beginning between now and 2020. As my colleague and friend, David Foot, of the University of Toronto, quipped in his bestselling book *Boom, Bust and Echo*[1]: "Demographics explain about two-thirds of everything."

39

The Golden Age

The notable phenomenon of the years 1960 to 1980 was the mass entry of baby boomers into the workplace. During that period, the number of workers earning a salary and paying taxes grew at a breathtaking rate. The Canadian welfare state expanded rapidly. We successively implemented hospital insurance, health insurance, low-cost college and university education, social services, public pension plans, more generous old age pensions, and employment benefits, etc. It was the Golden Age of social programs. Do you admire the politicians of the era—Pearson, Trudeau, Douglas, Robarts, Lesage, etc.—for developing our great social programs? You are right in so doing, for they were great people. But remember that from a financial perspective they had an easy time. Money was no problem. The huge addition to the tax revenue from the baby boomers was great food for their imagination.

The Flip Side

In the years to come, we are going to experience the flip side. Baby boomers born between 1945 and 1960 are today between forty-eight and sixty-three years old. In twelve years, in 2020, they will be sixty to seventy-five years old. Most of them will have begun their retirement. Just as they entered the job market en masse between 1960 and 1980, they will leave it in large numbers between now and 2025. Few will be participating in the labour force, and they will not be paying many taxes. (Okay, the money they will be withdrawing from their RRSP will be taxable, but that really will not change the overall picture.) The consequence is obvious: Our governments will be cash-strapped!

1. Less tax revenues

This year, 2008, 51 per cent of Canada's total population is working. In 2020, when the baby boomers' departure will be under way, only 49 per cent of the population will be working if the employment rates by age remain stable. The overall employment rate will thus have dropped two points from fifty-one. It will therefore be 4 per cent lower than it would have been otherwise. This may look like a small decrease, but it will actually have important consequences for government tax revenues. Simply put, we can calculate how much tax revenue governments would have lost today, in 2008, if the number of taxpayers had suddenly dropped by 4 per cent. Given that Canadians will pay $520 billion in taxes this year, the answer is that tax collections would be $21 billion less (4 per cent of $520 billion). That's point number one.

2. More health-care spending

That's not all. The passage of this large group of baby boomers into their golden years will push the percentage of senior citizens sixty-five years of age and older from 13 per cent of the total population today to 18 per cent in 2020. Since a senior citizen costs on average five times more in terms of health care as compared to a younger adult, this population aging will exert upward pressure on provincial finances, above and beyond the already extremely rapid increase in spending over the past several years (on average 7 per cent per year since 2000).

Once again, a simple way to comprehend the magnitude of this financial pressure is to calculate the impact the demographic change would have on provincial health-care spending if it were instantly realized in 2008. This year, total public spending on health care will be about $121 billion, of which $55 billion will be for seniors and $66 billion for the rest of the population. If the share of seniors in total population were 18 per cent instead of 13 per cent, health-care spending for them would increase to $76 billion. Meanwhile, other Canadians would account for 82 per cent of total population instead of 87 per cent, which would entail a reduction of health-care spending for them to $62 billion. The net outcome is that overall public spending for health care would be $138 billion instead of $121 billion. The additional pressure on (mainly) provincial finances would therefore have amounted to $17 billion. That's point number two.

3. More payments to seniors
Another government program that is going to suffer the effects of the aging baby boomer population is federal payments to seniors, including the venerable old-age pension and the guaranteed income supplement for low-income seniors. With 13 per cent of the population currently sixty-five years of age or older, the federal government expects to spend $33 billion in payments to seniors in 2008. If this percentage were to jump five points to 18 per cent immediately in 2008, as is in fact expected for the year 2020, Ottawa would have to come up with $12 billion more this year (five-thirteenths of $33 billion). That's point number three.

4. Possible savings

Will the aging of the Canadian population allow at least some savings? Yes, in the areas of children's benefits, childcare allowances, and education funding. According to the average birthrate and immigration scenarios put out by Statistics Canada, the relative weight of young people (birth to nineteen years old) in total population will drop by 13 per cent between 2008 and 2020. School enrolment will decline accordingly. This will permit proportional reductions in federal children's benefits and in provincial education and daycare spending. Now, in 2008, the combined value of all these expenditures on behalf of children and students is about $80 billion. If these expenses dropped suddenly by 13 per cent, governments would save $10 billion (13 per cent of $80 billion). That's point number four.

Will the demographic transition threaten the viability of our public pension plans? No. To avoid any slips due to demographic shockwaves, the various levels of government proactively revised the structure of the Canada Pension Plan and the Régime des rentes du Québec some time ago. The general contribution rate was upped to 9.9 per cent of insurable earnings in 2003. This rate will need only a slight increase later in this century to permit adequate financing for retirement income of baby boomers and their children for the foreseeable future.

The Tab: $40 Billion

Let's sum up. Baby boomers born between 1945 and 1960 are going to retire en masse, but they will leave few children and grandchildren behind them. Canada is thus going to undergo an important demographic transition. To highlight the financial consequences, I have presented a scenario that applied future reality to our current state of affairs. I have calculated the impact that demographic changes would have on public monies in Canada in 2008 if the age pyramid expected for 2020 suddenly applied today.

The result would be a marked deterioration of public finances. As we saw, tax revenues would drop by $21 billion; provincial spending on health care would increase by $17 billion; federal payments to seniors would rise by $12 billion; children's benefits, education spending, and childcare allowances could decrease by $10 billion. On net, if it were applied today, the age structure of 2020's population would make a $40-billion hole in government budgets for 2008; this would be split about evenly between the federal government and the provinces. In other words, there would be a new kind of "fiscal imbalance," demographic in nature. But this time it will hit Ottawa as hard as the provinces. Even worse, after 2020 the problem will not disappear; it will in fact get bigger, as baby boomers continue to retire in large numbers and fewer young adults enter the labour force.

After 2012, year after year, governments are going to see more and more disappointing tax revenues. The problem of health-care funding, which is already a thorny issue today, will become dramatic as the baby boomers get older. Federal payments to seniors will grow swiftly. While provinces may realize some savings in education, these will only partially compensate for the drop in tax revenue and increased health-care spending. There is one silver lining: Our public pension plans will weather the demographic transition without too much difficulty.

Financially, governments have three options: go back into debt (the Japanese approach), cut or privatize public services (the U.S. approach), or raise taxes (the Swedish approach). Each government will choose the combination that best matches its political philosophy. In Ottawa, just as in the provinces, we cannot exclude the possibility of a new cycle of debt. A funding crisis could lead, more quickly than one might think, to a major overhaul of our cherished public health-care system. This would no doubt include increased participation of the private sector in health-care management and delivery. And from now on we had better forget about further major tax reductions.

Growth and Solidarity

Governments can implement two main kinds of policies to deal with the demographic transition: a policy of economic growth and a policy of "intergenerational solidarity." They can accelerate economic growth in the usual ways: fight unemployment and poverty, encourage employment of older workers, accelerate the integration of immigrant workers and foster education, entrepreneurship, savings, investment, innovation, and productivity. Stronger economic growth would reduce the effects of overall economic decline and tax revenue losses following retirement of the baby boomers.

Governments could also attempt to protect new generations from debt, program spending cuts, and tax hikes by convincing current generations to proactively share the tab. This policy of solidarity between generations could be based either on accelerated repayment of public debt, or on building up a transitional "generations fund"—as it is called in Quebec—to be spent later when the demographic transition is in full swing. A reduction of debt or the building of a generations fund would be financed by today's taxpayers. It would aim at reducing the tax burden of tomorrow's taxpayers, leaving them with more money to access the same level of public services as today. Intergenerational solidarity here would mean that, after having treated themselves to a great party, baby boomers would not want to leave all the cleanup duties to their children.

Two governments in Canada have followed this intergenerational solidarity path: the federal government and the Alberta government. For several years now, each federal budget has set aside a sum to repay part of the debt. For its part, Edmonton has followed in Norway's footsteps in building its Heritage Fund and reimbursing its debt through oil and gas royalties.

Other governments could follow their lead. Quebec, Manitoba, and British Columbia could sell their electricity at prices closer to continental market prices rather than massively subsidizing provincial consumption. As well as being ecological, such a move would free up money to repay provincial debt or invest in a generations fund. There is an obvious political obstacle to overcome: It is difficult to take the gift of cheap electricity away from taxpayers who are so used to it. However, the stakes are high: to protect our children from otherwise un-avoidable and sizable program cuts, tax increases, and debt.

Procrastination Trap

Those who think the above analysis is unduly alarmist—apocalyptic—are wrong. The passage of baby boomers to old age is not weather forecasting. It is certain. And the amount of the tab that they are going to leave us with is both large and unavoidable—at least for anyone who has not forgotten how to cross-multiply. Our generation is responsible for recognizing the problem, creating solutions, and sharing the cost in an equitable manner. However, it is far from clear at this time that we will be going this way. It will be difficult to convince baby boomers to deal with the demographic problem effectively and in a timely fashion. Demographic change is slow and in-sidious, not massive and sudden like a hurricane or a flood. The temptation will always be there to postpone action to to-morrow, all the more so because those who will suffer from inaction are not ourselves, but future generations. But pro-crastination conceals a trap: It will only make the problem that has to be solved bigger over time. There is danger ahead.

Notes

1. Written with Daniel Stoffman (Toronto: Macfarlane Walter & Ross, 1996, page 2).

WHITHER THE CANADIAN ECONOMY?

BY DON DRUMMOND

MANUFACTURING ACCOUNTS FOR 15 per cent of Canada's output and is a source of well-paying jobs. The sequence of the Free Trade Agreement, the North American Free Trade Agreement, the lapsing of the Auto Pact, and then the termination of import quotas in the textile and clothing industries sent a message that the sector would have to stand on its own two feet in competition with the United States, Mexico, and many other countries. Now a new source of competition has arisen from China and other emerging Asian economies. Simultaneously the sector must cope with a strong Canadian dollar due to sky-high commodity prices. Can Canada's industrial base prosper in the face of these challenges, or will it whither by 2020? Will manufacturing wages be driven down to the low levels some of our competitors pay?

Heightened international competition is most acute for Canada's manufacturing sector, and that means the story largely revolves around Ontario and Quebec. In those provinces manufacturing accounts for about 19 per cent of total output, nearly double the average in the other eight provinces. On the surface the economies of these central Canadian provinces—Ontario's in particular—appear to be in good shape and have weathered the transition to free trade quite well. Only three regions have a higher standard of living than Ontario's if we consider peer regions of similar size. Quebec fares worse with a standard of living smack in the middle of the thirty developed economies in the Organization for Co-operation and Development (OECD). Yet the relatively poor productivity records of both economies suggest all is not well. In a comparison with the fourteen U.S. competitor states of equal or larger populations, Ontario's Institute for Competitiveness and Prosperity finds that Ontario and Quebec make unfortunate bedfellows at the bottom of the pile. Ontario's real GDP per capita was $6,000 below the median in 2006 and Quebec's fared even worse with a $13,000 deficiency. For both provinces inferior productivity is the main culprit.

Our best estimate is that output per hour in the Canadian private sector is only 79 per cent that in the United States. So, with the Canadian dollar recently trading around parity with the U.S. dollar, there is a strain on the competitiveness of Canadian manufacturing. In response, manufacturers have shed labour, cutting 18 per cent of the sector's jobs in Ontario and 21 per cent in Quebec since November 2002. A large number of U.S. factory workers, particularly in the south, are accepting very low wages with few benefits, and this adds an additional competitiveness threat. We could call this the "Delphi effect." When workers of this giant U.S. auto-parts company worked for General Motors, their base wage was around $40 per hour. It went to $27 when Delphi was hived off. Now the company wants to cut the base wage to $16.50 when it comes out of bankruptcy protection, and it is seeking major concessions on benefits. It is hard to imagine that this downward pressure on wages will not spread to other parts of manufacturing and into Canada.

A new front of competitive pressure is coming from Asian economies such as China. Canada's trade balance in manufactured goods with China has deteriorated by over 1 per cent of GDP over the past decade. Import penetration from China no longer consists of just lower-value-added goods such as T-shirts and simple toys. The strongest increases have come in machinery and mechanical goods. The deterioration has hit the Ontario economy hardest, with an increase in the deficit with China of over 2 per cent of Ontario's GDP, and most of that is in goods classified as capital intensive. Quebec has suffered only a minor deterioration in its trade balance with China in manufactured products, but that has not spared it from a significant deterioration in other goods and with other countries.

This is not the first time an advanced economy has faced a new competitiveness threat from an emerging economy. The United Kingdom has been through this many times with former colonies, most notably the rise of the U.S. economic empire. Yet the U.K. economy is still one of the wealthiest in the world. Japan went from 29 per cent of U.S. real per capita incomes in 1950 to exceeding the U.S. level by 1986 and comprising one-quarter of all U.S. imports. Many proclaimed that the U.S. would soon cede its economic supremacy to Japan. Yet this did not happen, as output per capita has grown twice as fast in the United States since the early 1990s as in Japan. In general, advanced economies have shifted away from goods towards services and picked niches where their productivity advantage is greatest. And, as in the U.S. case, the competition spurred a rise in productivity in the wealthier economy. Another facet of the adjustment was that rising incomes in the emerging economies provided an outlet for the goods and services of the wealthiest countries.

A skeptic could say that previous experiences, showing wins for both developed and emerging economies, may not be relevant. By embracing free trade and foreign investment, providing incentives for the rapid integration of leading-edge technologies, and massively investing in education and infrastructure, the emerging economies are reaping the benefits of the capital and brains of the advanced economies at lightning speed. Since 1997 the cumulative productivity gains in Korea, China, and India have been 112, 102, and 87 per cent respectively, while Canada stands at a lowly 15 per cent. Even the United States outpaced us at 28 per cent. Real per capita incomes have risen more than 750 per cent in China and almost tripled in India since 1980, but so far that has not benefited Canadian exports. All the emerging economies are aiming production at a pretty high rung on the value-added ladder, and some, like India, are formidable competitors in key service industries.

Advanced economies like Canada's have sufficient financial and resource wealth that part of the adjustment process could be that the emerging economies use their huge surplus savings to purchase our assets, and we use the proceeds to maintain our consumption standards. But surely we have greater aspirations than this. We must strive to stay at the top of the world economic order with ample, well-paying jobs matched to strong growth in output. And that comes down to productivity. An economy can only sustain high wages if it has strong productivity.

In order to remedy the productivity woes of the Canadian economy, we first need to understand how the process works. The conventional view is that productivity rises as existing firms and workers figure out smarter ways of doing things. But work by Statistics Canada shows that less than half of productivity gains come in this way. The main source of productivity growth is the competitive process that shifts market share toward plants—either existing or new—that are more productive. The pace of market-share reallocation has increased since the Free Trade Agreement. Between 1973 and 1997, 37 per cent of market share in a manufacturing industry was transferred from plants that either contracted or closed, to new plants or plants that expanded. Employment in manufacturing is just as dynamic as output. Over a decade, two out of every five jobs in manufacturing are eliminated because of plant closures or downsizing and replaced by new jobs. Looking across sub-categories of manufacturing, Statistics Canada found that a lack of investment in new establishments differentiates the more dynamic industries from the declining ones.

International experience shows that success in driving up productivity comes from combinations of greater trade liberalization, strong investment increases, better education, and, above all, rapid change. But change can be uncomfortable, and it disproportionately imposes a cost on the least-educated and least-skilled. So it is important that, while fostering change, there be supportive mechanisms for those most adversely affected.

From this context we can set out a recipe for raising productivity in Canada and in particular its industrial base in Ontario and Quebec. It should first be noted that some things have been going right on this front in recent years. Productivity in Canadian manufacturing has risen at an annual pace of 3 per cent since 2003. That now needs to be sustained and strengthened.

Canadian firms need to invest more, particularly in machinery and equipment, where our stock per hour worked is only 55 per cent that in the United States. Now is an excellent time, because the rise in the external value of the Canadian dollar has slashed the cost of imported capital. Governments have taken steps to lower the effective tax rates on business investment. Canada's ranking within the OECD is set to improve significantly by 2012. Ontario and Quebec could reduce their general corporate income-tax rates further. Furthermore, both need to reduce marginal personal income-tax rates which, at almost 50 per cent for high-income workers and effectively much higher for modest-income families, dull the incentives to work, save, and invest. Both governments have appropriately been ramping up investments in education and infrastructure in recent years and need to continue. With an ageing population, which is particularly worrying in Quebec because of its low birth rate, immigration will be the source of most labour-force growth. The provinces must work with the federal government to improve the economic benefits of immigration. This needs to go beyond the recent focus on facilitating credential recognition and settlement services to include more pro-active marketing to potential immigrants best fitting the profiles of skill shortages. Companies and individuals in Ontario need to devote more time and money to lifelong learning and training. Both provinces need to complete the adjustment to market pricing on electricity and encourage new supply to limit price increases.

Ontario and Quebec each have specific challenges that need to be addressed in order to ensure prosperity in 2020. Exports account for 65 per cent of Ontario's real GDP, and the bulk of that passes through only three Ontario-U.S. border crossings. Congestion with long delays has long been a fact of life at these crossings. But with growing security concerns, the situation could get even worse. Governments are allocating money and personnel to alleviate the situation, but the question remains whether the response will be fast enough. Even if all goes to plan there will not be another crossing at the critical Windsor-Detroit link until 2013. Some administrative procedures like NEXUS and FAST to pre-clear low risk crossings appear promising on paper, but the take-up has been low. A free-flowing border is at the heart of the NAFTA promise. Without that, companies will not have the confidence that they can gain access to all North American markets from a Canadian base. Ontario will have increasing difficulty attracting new investment and risks, losing some it already has.

At the same time as manufacturers are being given the message they have to stand on their own two feet in open competition, the Ontario economy and its taxpayers are handicapped by a net fiscal drag from the federal government as part of its redistributive role. As Quebec is a net recipient of federal transfers, this issue puts Ontario's and Quebec's interests in conflict. For 2005, Statistics Canada estimates that the federal government extracted $20.1 billion more in taxes from Ontario taxpayers than it spent in the province. That amounted to a fiscal drag of 3.8 per cent of Ontario's economy, whereas, excluding Alberta, the other provinces had a net federal fiscal injection of 4 per cent. Similarly, most U.S. states have a net fiscal injection from their federal government. The point is not that federal governments should run deficits. Rather, it is to ponder how much redistribution the taxpayers of provinces with above-average incomes can finance when they need to be competitive not only with other jurisdictions in Canada but with the rest of the world as well. The current situation also makes it difficult for the Ontario government to finance the services its residents and businesses need at competitive tax rates. In 2005, Ontario received $1,235 per capita less in federal transfers than the median of all provinces. Its own source revenues were virtually bang on the median, but, excluding resource revenues, they were almost 10 per cent above the median due to a combination of fairly high tax rates and strong incomes. The balancing item was that Ontario spent $1,109 less than the provincial median, putting it in tenth, or last, place among provinces. Education was one of the components that ended up in that last place standing, compromising the province's ability to meet its competitiveness challenges.

Quebec's particular fiscal challenge is its debt burden, which per capita is the second-highest in Canada, and relative to income is among the highest in the world. The cost of financing that debt leaves Quebecers facing one of the highest tax burdens in Canada and impedes public initiatives that could bolster productivity. The recent commitment to reduce the absolute level of the debt burden is to be commended. Progress needs to be made soon, because Quebec's labour force could come to a standstill by 2020. Its population has been growing at only half the rate of the rest of Canada, and the gap is even wider with the United States. Quebec cannot raise its already high personal and corporate income taxes, but it should examine raising the cost of some public services, such as cutting subsidies to electricity and post-secondary education and raising some consumption taxes.

Ontario and Quebec have recently made some positive moves to address competitiveness challenges. Both are phasing out their capital taxes. This was the most damaging form of taxation to economic growth. Ontario is also reducing the education portion of provincial property taxes. Quebec has taken a stab at reducing its heavy personal-income-tax burden. Ontario will soon need to address its corporate income tax rate, which is now considerably higher than in competing provinces. It must also reform its antiquated retail sales tax, which gathers about 40 per cent of its revenue from business inputs, including capital.

History suggests that advanced economies like Canada's not only survive but actually benefit from emerging competitors. That may be particularly difficult to pull off between now and 2020 in the case of Canada's industrial base in Ontario and Quebec. The key will be whether they can bolster their dismal records on productivity. That may not be a sufficient condition, but we do know it is necessary. Attention is being paid to this requirement, but the fire seems to be missing. Somebody had better light the match soon.

THE UNITED NATIONS
IN DECLINE

BY JENNIFER WELSH

Below is a story of what could be, unless new ideas—and new leadership—are infused into the UN.

AUGUST 1, 2020 (NEW YORK)—Canada's ambassador to the United Nations, Jasmine Basran, is taping up the last of her boxes as the movers empty out her large office on Manhattan's Second Avenue. "We just couldn't justify such a large space when our mission to the UN has been so reduced." There was barely a whimper in Canada when the Department of Foreign Affairs announced in 2018 that staffing for Canada's Permanent Mission to the United Nations in New York would be cut from more than thirty to fewer than ten. "Our diplomatic presence now needs to be concentrated elsewhere, particularly at the Canadian mission to NATO in Brussels," Basran explains.

Earlier in the day, the ambassador gave us a tour of the UN Security Council chamber, which looks more like a museum than a forum for active diplomacy. The council hasn't met in more than a year due to the deadlock over Syria's testing of an intercontinental ballistic missile. Ever since the U.S. campaign to give newly independent Taiwan a non-permanent seat on the Security Council, there has been virtually no possibility of the Permanent Members agreeing to collective action. China, backed by Russia, vetoes most of the resolutions proposed by the United States and the European Union. Japan and India, the two new semi-permanent members of the council (added during the reform conference of 2012) also tend to be divided on U.S.-inspired initiatives.

Basran, however, seems philosophical about the council's lack of activity. "The council was also marginalized during the Cold War. The 1990s were in many ways the exception rather than the rule. Really, for the past decade, the action has been happening elsewhere for Canada—especially in the wake of our big push in Afghanistan. NATO is now the primary focus of Canada's international diplomacy."

What a dramatic change from thirty years ago, when commentators everywhere were proclaiming the death of NATO after the fall of communism. NATO's original purpose, as a diplomat once quipped, had been to "keep the U.S. in, the Germans down, and the Russians out." But without the Soviet bloc to serve as an external enemy for the western alliance, NATO was expected to crumble and give way to a revitalized UN.

Today, this prediction looks like a quaint piece of history. NATO has continued its process of expansion, which began in 1999 with the admission of the Czech Republic, Hungary, and Poland, and continued with the addition of ten countries over the following decade. The latest successful applicants—Bosnia, Georgia, and Ukraine—have brought the total number in the alliance up to thirty-two. Throughout the process, the United States has pursued its objective of transforming NATO into a global forum for democracies, which can act collectively to promote democratic values among and beyond its members.

NATO has also proved that it can intervene more quickly in trouble spots around the globe. Its Council for Peace and Security, created in 2012, has at its disposal a contingent of troops from each member state that can be sent abroad for humanitarian missions.

For Canadians, the transition to this new world has been difficult and confusing. In a 2004 poll conducted by the Dominion Institute, just after the breakdown in diplomacy over the Iraq War, almost three-quarters of Canadians said the UN was still a better venue in which Canada could make a difference in the world than alternative, regional organizations. Far from being a sign of the UN's failure, Canadians believed the crisis over Iraq demonstrated the pitfalls that would face countries if they acted without UN support.

For seventy years, Canada was a staunch and consistent supporter of the UN's multilateral mechanisms, and was at one time the seventh largest donor to the UN and one of the major troop-contributing countries to UN peacekeeping. Indeed, this last area of activity was a dominant component of the Canadian national identity during the second half of the twentieth century. But this self-image has undergone significant evolution.

Long used to thinking of themselves as the "world's peace-keepers," who rarely fire a gun, Canadians over the past two decades have watched their men and women in uniform engage in direct and fierce combat in the countryside and towns of Afghanistan. (In fact, as many Canadians predicted during the row over our involvement in Afghanistan in 2008, there is still a small contingent of Canadian troops in southern Afghanistan today.) At the same time, the country's participation in UN peacekeeping operations continued to decline after 2000—partly as a result of a shortage of Canadian human resources, but also due to the fact that more developing countries provide the horsepower for peacekeeping and peace-building missions.

It has taken some time for Canadians to relinquish their hopes and dreams for the UN. In 2010, the vast majority still would have agreed with the words of their former prime minister, Lester Pearson, who described the UN as "our best, and perhaps our last, hope of bringing about a creative peace if mankind is to end a savage tradition that the strong do what they can and the weak suffer what they must." But these dreams were already beginning to look unrealistic in September 2005, when leaders from around the globe converged at the Sixtieth Anniversary Summit of the UN in New York.

Despite some positive changes, the summit failed to reinvigorate the UN after its painful experiences during the Iraq War and the scandals associated with the oil-for-food program. This failure was mainly a consequence of unreasonably high expectations—raised in particular by former secretary general Kofi Annan's reform rhetoric prior to the summit. Annan heralded the gathering of leaders as a "once-in-a-generation" opportunity to transform the UN from a body established out of the ashes of World War II into a forum that could manage the challenges of the twenty-first century.

Leaders salvaged an agreement and posed for the cameras. Then–prime minister Paul Martin proclaimed at the time that "Canada cannot conceive of a world succeeding without the

United Nations." In the end, the negotiations did not succeed in building a consensus on a new conception of collective security—one that could encapsulate both the threats from weapons proliferation and the human catastrophe of under-development.

The summit's outcome only deepened the divisions between the developing world and the developed world (particularly the United States), and made ongoing discussions about the UN's role in the world even more fractious. Powerful developed states continued to fear that the UN would not act decisively on the threats that concerned them (terrorism, weapons of mass destruction, and transnational crime), while developing countries continued to insist that the greatest threats to their security resided elsewhere—in poverty, infectious disease, and collapsing state structures.

The first sign of malaise for the UN came with the failure to agree on a budget in 2008. This left the new secretary-general, Ban Ki-moon, without the resources needed to support ongoing UN peacekeeping missions in Liberia, Ivory Coast, Haiti, Burundi, and Sudan. Anyone reading the tea leaves could have predicted this impending train wreck. A majority of developing countries (led by the G77 and China) set up a roadblock to much-needed management reforms of the UN by refusing to approve the secretary-general's reform proposals. But the United States had linked its backing for the budget to progress on these improvements in the UN's management and administration. The stage was set for a confrontation.

The crisis intensified over the next two years with the disastrous end to the UN peacekeeping mission in Darfur. It had taken a great deal of diplomatic pressure for the secretary-general to persuade the Sudanese government to accept twenty thousand UN personnel on its territory to replace the mission of the African Union. By the time the UN finally took over, on December 31, 2007, the international community had managed to mobilize only half of what was needed. Ban Ki-moon's calls for more men, and more equipment, continued to fall on deaf ears. By the end of 2008, a total of three hundred thousand civilians had died and close to three million were forced from their homes. In addition, the slow lead-up to an international deployment allowed Islamic militants in the region to mobilize, creating an environment of extreme danger for foreign troops. After a disastrous showdown in the spring of 2009 in which more than a thousand peacekeepers were killed, troop-donating countries airlifted their soldiers out of the country.

The final blow came in 2010, when Ban Ki-moon's term of office was not renewed due to diplomatic confrontation between the United States and China. That left the secretary-general's office unfilled for two years. Hopes were raised when a candidate who could garner universal support was nominated, former Afghan president Hamid Karzai. But only four months after he was installed in 2012, he was assassinated by Taliban terrorists.

That year saw the UN descend into an existential crisis. For a time it appeared as though its member states might rally. Encouragingly, states such as Germany, Brazil, and South Africa set aside their ambitions for Security Council membership, and allowed a more modest proposal for council reform (which added two new semi-permanent members and five new non-permanent members) to be endorsed by the General Assembly. But the UN has never really recovered from the events of 2008–2012, and the frontal assault on its vocation as a force for global peace and dialogue.

For so long, the biggest factor working in favour of the UN was the lack of alternatives. Defenders of the organization, when faced with criticism, would commonly reply: "If the United Nations didn't exist, it would have to be invented." After 2012, this rationale began to lose its punch. Even in the realm of poverty reduction and health, alternative organizations and actors (particularly private foundations) began to outstrip the UN in terms of both funding and effectiveness. Without commitment, leadership, and new ideas from its member states, the UN could not maintain its status at the top of the global multilateral hierarchy.

Meanwhile, regional bodies were growing in strength and finding faster, more effective ways to engage in collective action. The Association of Southeast Asian Nations, the African Union, and the Gulf Cooperation Council followed NATO's lead in developing co-operative approaches to security and defence. Today, an ad hoc body has been established to facilitate dialogue among these regional organizations on global crises.

On the economic, health, and environmental fronts, the new L20 (Leaders 20, an expansion on the old G8) has taken centre stage as a forum for managing global financial matters, threats to the environment, and potential outbreaks of infectious disease. Canada has been particularly active in this innovative body, and is playing a constructive bridging role between developed and developing countries.

All of these organizations operate with a lighter "footprint" than the UN, and have thus far been able to avoid the failures of management and oversight that dogged the UN during the first decade of this century. But then again, none of these regional alternatives is driven by the ambition and hope that characterized the founding fathers of the United Nations.

The more historically minded among us still think back wistfully to 1945, and the "spirit of San Francisco." Could such a spirit be revived again to breathe new life into the United Nations?

Before we could hope for a new "San Francisco," we would need a new "Dumbarton Oaks"—the meeting at which the Allied powers came together to agree upon a global vision and to lead the process of change. But this looks unlikely today. The scheme for the UN worked, according to the great historian Paul Kennedy, because the bigger and wealthier powers realized they had to be "providers" of international security for others. At the moment, this leadership and engagement from the great powers is lacking. So, too, is a collective sense of responsibility or a consensus among them about the most important security challenges facing the international community. The United States, as so many predicted two decades ago, is no longer the unrivalled superpower. And the new great powers, China, India, and Brazil, have yet to define their global vision.

In the meantime, the Canadian government is decorating its new suite of offices on the Rue de la Régence in Brussels and sending the high-profile Justin Trudeau to serve as ambassador to NATO.

THE CURSE OF ALBERTA

BY ROGER GIBBINS

IT SHOULD NEVER have come to this. Tomorrow Albertans will go to the polls to vote on leaving Canada, and any doubt as to the outcome was removed last month when the British Columbia legislature resolved to hold a similar referendum within six months. It is likely that Saskatchewan will soon follow suit.

The legal technicalities are straightforward. Back in the late 1990s, when the Quebec sovereignty movement was still alive and well, the Supreme Court and later Parliament, through the *Clarity Act*, recognized that the Government of Canada has an obligation to enter into negotiations if there is a clear expression of the will of the population of a province on whether the province should cease to be a part of Canada and become an independent state. Those negotiations could begin as early as next week.

Back in the 1990s, no one imagined that this option would be exercised by a province other than Quebec. The critical question, therefore, is how did we get to this sorry state of affairs? What went so wrong along the way?

Although there has always been a small smattering of separatist support in Alberta, usually a very small smattering, the origins of our current mess date back to 2006, when oil prices first passed $70 a barrel. The Alberta government, having paid off its provincial debt, was then generating larger surpluses than the federal government.

At the same time, the Ontario economy was beginning to falter in the face of both intensifying international competition and weakening American markets. A rising Canadian dollar, driven upwards by robust international markets for western Canadian natural resources, squeezed the vise even tighter on the traditional manufacturing sector.

For a while the growing regional divide was masked. On average, the Canadian economy was doing well, and thus regional disparities within the context of more general national prosperity attracted less attention. Unemployment rates were at record lows, and Canadians across the country were enjoying growing real estate wealth.

It was also assumed by most Canadians that the regional disparities being generated by Alberta's energy wealth, and for that matter by the general wealth of the resource-based western Canadian economy, would largely disappear once resource markets returned to normal levels. The western boom was seen as a temporary blip, a one-off windfall, analogous to a lottery win. As then–Alberta premier Ralph Klein noted when asked about high energy prices, "what goes up must come down," which indeed had been the historical experience of Alberta's volatile boom and bust economy.

Thus Canadians waited patiently, or in some cases impatiently, for energy prices to return to normal, and for the natural order of things to reassert itself. Over time, however, it began to sink in that the new normal was $70 oil, and then $80, $90, $100, and higher. The good old days of cheap energy, and with them the older model of the Canadian economy, were gone, along with hot airline meals.

Now, of course, the Canadian economy was not alone in being hit by higher energy prices, and indeed in some ways it was better off than most, given that Canada was a net exporter of oil, natural gas, uranium, and hydro-electric power. The problem and the political crisis came from the unequal regional distribution of those resources.

Slowly it became clear that the accumulation of wealth in Alberta, and to a lesser degree across the West, was the new reality. At the same time, the Ontario economy continued to be squeezed by competitors from China and India, by American protectionism in the face of the same competition, and by weakening American markets as the United States grappled unsuccessfully with growing debt, a deteriorating balance of payments, and international obligations that could not be shed.

In response, the western provinces were scrambling to find ways by which regional wealth could be used to positive national effect. The Alberta government, for example, generously endowed the Canadian Scholarship Fund, to the point at which it dwarfed the Rhodes and Woodrow Wilson funds and was attracting the best and the brightest international students to universities across the country.

Similar endowments for sustainable energy, clean coal, wellness programs, and medical research were pushing Canada to the forefront of the international community. Canada, led by the western provinces, was shedding its historical underperformance in the commercialization of university research. Furthermore, the western provinces collaborated to strengthen transportation linkages between Canada and the booming Asia Pacific economies, with positive effects that rippled across the country from sea to sea to sea.

And, in Alberta, the onslaught of prosperity gave residents both the opportunity and the luxury to manage the impact of energy developments on an increasingly stressed provincial land base. The pace of development was brought within the carrying capacity of the physical environment, and the province's vast energy endowment was not being exploited at the expense of its natural capital.

These steps, however, could moderate but not bridge the growing regional divide in the national economy. As oil prices crept past $100 a barrel then $110, and then $120, the divide became even deeper. Every escalation brought more wealth to the West, and more cost-pressure to central Canadian firms. As energy prices continued their inexorable climb, the regional imbalance grew in step, and all this took place against the backdrop of a troubled American economy.

There was no question that the regional concentration of energy wealth was a source of strain for the federation, as Ontario and Quebec faced significant out-migration of people and head offices, and immigration became more difficult to attract. Not surprisingly, therefore, a political reaction was inevitable.

Although the western-led national government argued gamely that what was good for the Alberta economy was also good for the Canadian economy, the political battle was lost to a coalition of opposition parties running under the banner "Canadian resources for Canadians."

The equalization formula, funded as it was by federal tax-payers, the great bulk of whom lived outside Alberta and even outside the West, provided little counterweight for the public wealth that was piling up in Alberta. The province's Heritage Savings and Trust Fund, now worth well more than $150 billion, made Alberta an easy target.

Shortly before the pivotal election, renewed military conflict in the Middle East, nuclear weapons testing by Iran, and an outbreak of civil war in the Russian Caucuses drove oil prices close to $200 a barrel. Despite a surge of migration into the West, the majority of the national electorate still lived in Ontario and Quebec, and swept into power a new government determined to arrest and even turn back the energy-led tide of prosperity in western Canada.

Many in the West, particularly those with relatives, friends, and business colleagues living in other parts of Canada, had some sympathy for "Canadian resources for Canadians." Western Canadians, after all, were enjoying a great deal of prosperity, and thus the change in the national government alone was not enough to push them over the national unity edge.

Unfortunately, things did not go well politically. The new federal government, led by Ontario's first prime minister in more than fifty years, introduced a draconian series of tax measures to channel energy wealth into the national treasury. The need to address global warming was used as the rationale for sweeping carbon taxes, but the regional redistribution of wealth was the real driver.

Constitutional niceties were put aside as the federal government's responsibility for peace, order, and good government was expanded to include the responsibility to reduce regional disparities. Energy resources, it turned out, although not hydro resources, were now in the national interest and under the jurisdictional umbrella of the federal government.

Even then, Albertans were not pushed to the breaking point. The straw that finally broke the province's back was the environmental disaster unleashed by federal management of Alberta's resource endowment. The province was quite literally out of sight and out of mind, and, as the price of oil approached $200 a barrel, the focus of the national government shifted to more and more production. The collapse of an increasingly fragile environment and the destruction of iconic landscapes were seen as an unfortunate but unavoidable price to pay as the rest of the country used petrodollars as a shield to protect their economies from ever-intensifying international competition.

In short, Alberta became the Canadian cash cow, the bulwark against the economic effects of international competition and weak American markets. Energy revenues were used to prop up an increasingly unproductive manufacturing economy, with petrodollars becoming the new tariff wall. In the near term, Canadians were therefore able to avoid the painful economic adjustments that other countries had to endure in the face of high energy prices, but in the long term the national economy was further weakened.

It turned out, of course, that while the concentration of energy wealth in one province had dramatic effects, the distribution of that wealth across a much larger national population had correspondingly more limited effects. The expectations held by supporters of "Canadian resources for Canadians" could only be met if energy production was pushed higher and higher, and pushed beyond the carrying capacity of the Alberta environment.

Environmental protection comes first and foremost from those who can taste, see, touch, and breathe environmental degradation, and not from distant bureaucrats or voters. This meant that as control of Alberta's resource endowment shifted from provincial to national hands, concerns about environmental damage weakened. The standards of environmental stewardship and intergenerational equity that had come to shape the provincial policy architecture were abandoned by a national government intent on maximizing energy revenues.

The result was the emergence of a new and powerful political coalition in Alberta determined to lead Alberta out of Canada. Environmentalists locked arms with energy producers in defence of the province; ideologically moderate urbanities joined forces with ranchers and farmers as both urban and rural environments became even more stressed. "Canadian resources for Canadians" came to be seen as environmental degradation for Alberta, and thus the fight was joined to save both the provincial economy and environment.

And now, in 2020, where do we stand as Albertans prepare to go to the polls, and to strike out on their own? The nation's energy wealth has been dispersed and dissipated without strategic impact; there is no legacy except for unsustainable regional transfers and social programming. Canada is trailing rather than leading the technological race to wean the global economy from its dependence on hydrocarbons. Alberta's population has shrunk as people fled a growing ecological disaster. And, ironically, the rest of the Canadian economy, buffered by energy revenues, is now even less able to compete globally.

The Alberta Camelot that began to emerge in 2006 has come and gone. It was the Canadian curse that the Camelot created by high energy prices was located "in the regions," that it came to be seen as a national threat rather than a national asset.

What, then, could we have done differently? We could have recognized that regional swings in the national economy are inevitable, and should be accommodated rather than resisted by public policies. We could have accelerated the transition to new energy sources instead of shielding Canadian industries and consumers from high energy prices. We could have built on the wisdom of "think globally, act locally" and recognized that the delicate balance between economic growth and environmental protection is better struck provincially rather than nationally. We could have built protections for regional interests and aspirations into the institutional architecture of the national government.

We could have done a lot, and instead we stand on the verge of losing so much. It should never have come to this.

NALUNAKTUQ: THE ARCTIC AS FORCE, INSTEAD OF RESOURCE

BY RACHEL A. QITSUALIK

In 2020, the white bear's tracks grace Arctic snows no longer. The remnants of Inuit culture kneel amid vernal invaders— grass, fronds, trees—weeping for lack of the ice they have always known. Factories sprawl like the nests of great, sickly birds; and ships, now more common than seals, ply oil-shadowed waters.

The histrionic paragraph above reflects an all-too-popular vision of the Arctic's future, often held by those who have never set foot beyond the tree-line. But I grew up in the Arctic. I've lived in various cities, too. I've bedded down in an iglu as comfortably as in a house; untangled sled traces as readily as catching the bus. And I know something of the differences between those places, so that my mind's eye too easily conjures possible futures. Some, I simply don't want to tell anybody about. But I can provide, for anyone who cares to peek, at least one such vision:

My teeth are blue, in the hot August of 2020, and my husband and I haven't managed to walk far. I can't seem to quit stooping for the wealth of blueberries. We look up, chuckling at the staccato noise of a raven, shortly before bird and laughter are subsumed beneath the roar of vehicles. Squinting under the sun's glare, we spot a trio of helicopters flying out over Frobisher Bay.

"Another CARE patrol," my husband says, pointing. "Too small for rescue."

I shake my head, unsure, since there are now as many rescue missions as so-called Canadian Arctic Regional Endeavours. The CARE acronym replaced the old SOVOP (Sovereignty Operation) around 2012 when the federal government decided it needed a friendlier term. I remember the first one—Operation Narwhal, in 2004—wherein vehicles were hobbled by unexpected frost, and the military had to call upon the assistance of Inuit Rangers after losing contact with two communications specialists in the hills. Those operations had improved significantly by 2010, however, in ample time to address our contemporary problem: foreign shipwrecks.

It is at once embarrassing and alarming, the way wrecks are piling up in the so-called Northwest Passage, those Arctic waters where Inuit have hunted for ages. They yet hunt out there, of course, since Inuit can hunt just as easily from boat as upon the once-common sea ice. It's tricky, navigating the sludge of icebergs in a small boat, but definitely worth it: global warming, it seems, has caused planktonic populations to rise, increasing the numbers of fish and sea mammals with easier access to waterways. I can't recall a time when the hunting culture was this strong, although bears are no longer sought after. Warmth has made the recently stabilized bear population more dangerous, since the animals are reverting to the coastal/island hunting style of their ancestors, but their numbers are nevertheless small. The end of the bear hunt is no real loss (especially to me), and many overlook it in light of the sea's increased bounty.

Unfortunately for many, another variety of prospective boom is increasingly resembling bust. It's amazing to think back on all that sabre-rattling among the United States, Denmark, and Canada, over rights to the Northwest Passage, only to have so many ships ripped asunder by unanticipated icebergs. In 2018, there was great deal of huzzah over Canada's finalized licensing system (favouring the U.S., of course) for foreign usage of Canadian Arctic waters, even though the U.S. had already been using the waters for some time. The issue only came to the forefront of public awareness in 2011, when an American oil tanker (the *Rose of Texas*, or something like that) was split open three hundred kilometres from Gjoa Haven, ruining local fish stocks and poisoning coastlines. Inuit made little headway in complaining that the bacterial strain used to clean up the oil was giving their children skin ulcerations, though the Canadian public at least organized a relief effort once pictures of afflicted seal pups came out. The result was the licensing system of two years ago, along with heavy costs in CARE operations to make sure that no illegal dumping, immigration, speculation, or fishing occurs. Add to that the cost of rescue efforts to foreign ships, ever dashing themselves like dazed juggernauts upon this new and unfathomable Arctic.

The Land, you see (as Inuit call the Arctic), has always liked to play tricks. In this case, all the profiteers were so busy expecting Arctic waters to dutifully refrain from solidifying that they forgot one thing: the pole is still far from ice-free, and the tellurian warming goes on. As ice farther north warms and breaks off, the resultant "slush"—ice-chunks anywhere from the size of a baseball to that of a high-rise—float south. Instead of the expected, ice-free "Northwest Passage," the Danish tankers shipping fresh water from Greenland (there is, after all, a global freshwater crisis in 2020), and the U.S. tankers shipping (what else?) oil, have instead found themselves negotiating a treacherous, boreal labyrinth.

So many lives have already been ruined as a result of greed and lack of foresight; but that, too, is an old story in the Arctic. I pick an Arctic dandelion (a plant that someone, the other day, snippily insisted to me was not native to the Arctic, though it is), and I turn to the town of Iqaluit, the edge of whose sprawl lies nearby. The housing crisis of years past is over for now, having been solved by development. The illusion of boom, of less permafrost and more shipping, lured hordes of southerners North more than a decade ago, believing that the Arctic was destined to become prime real estate amid rushes for gold, sapphires, and diamonds. They found, instead, an Arctic that was warmer, but nevertheless treeless and incapable of becoming any nation's new breadbasket, in which shipping costs and fair practices left a bitter taste in the mouths of the most rapacious companies. They built homes and complexes they were already fleeing by the time 2015 rolled around— homes that are now occupied by mostly Inuit families.

And as they retreated to the South again, pockets empty and lips curled, with bittersweet memories of a beautiful but strangely unprofitable Land, they were haunted by a single, frustrating mystery: The knowledge that they could never say exactly why the Arctic hadn't been what they'd expected.

But Inuit elders could have told them. If anyone had bothered to ask, Inuit might have explained the Land to them. And you can bet the word *nalunaktuq* would have been uttered.

Come back to the present, for a moment—even to a bit of the past.

The root word of *nalunaktuq* is *nalu*, or "without knowledge." In Inuktitut (the Inuit language, which is crammed with riddles), *nalunaktuq* loosely means "difficult to know" or "unpredictable." But why should the Inuit perspective on such a thing matter? Well, besides being the majority in the Arctic, the Land has already forced its harshest lessons upon them. And the best such lesson has been that of *nalunaktuq*: The fact that general trends serve as poor indicators of how the Arctic will actually behave. Many people understand that Inuit survivability and Land knowledge are one, but few suspect that both hinge upon acceptance of the Land's uncertain nature. Much of the popular shock over signs of warming in the Arctic stems from the assumption that, of all environments, the Arctic is traditionally the least inclined to change. This variety of pop sophism, however, is easily unmasked through even cursory examination of that era which birthed Inuit culture itself. For the truth is that Inuit were shaped by previous global warming.

The planet Earth, between AD 800 and AD 1200 was a hot place. There are tales of rich apple orchards in England, sunburns being common. As occurs at any time, in any place, when things begin to heat up, folks move about. History shows this to be one of the greatest eras of tribal migration and rise of empire. Inuit (or, archeologically, "Thule") first emerged out of Alaska, around the very time of the warm period's onset. The warmth had given sea mammals ready access to Canada's Arctic Archipelago, and Inuit culture had adapted to specialize in hunting them. They did so well that, by AD 1000 (the time of Leif Ericsson's discovery of Vinland), they had eaten their way across proto-Canada. By AD 1200 they were well settled into Greenland, just in time for the planet to go chilly again. Nevertheless, folklore—that subconscious history of a culture—rarely forgets: to this day, Inuit *ajaraaq* (string games) retain the pattern called Kigiaq. This is "The Beaver," an animal that once ranged as far as the Arctic, during the Earth's last warming period.

As heretical as it sounds, within the context of pop dogma, the last time the planet grew hotter, it was actually pretty good for Inuit. In part, this is because Inuit are adaptability itself, and other cultures who direct eyes toward the Arctic would do well to emulate such plasticity. Lately, we've become inundated with sweeping, nigh-hysterical declarations, along the lines of "Global warming will render 95 per cent of Arctic species extinct within ten years," or "Climate change will destroy Inuit culture within a decade." We humans instinctively love a crusade; but a crusade is past-oriented, while adaptation is future-oriented. We cannot trust crisis, since someone always profits from fear; nor can we trust prediction, until the day science can provide us with an accurate five-day forecast. But we humans, regardless of culture, can trust to our heritage as an ancient species, and an adaptive one. We can trust in our own ability to change, if the Land will not.

In truth, I fear more for southern folk than I do for Inuit. The common southern perception seems to be that global warming will reshape the North into the South, as though the Arctic were defined, up to this point, by cold alone. Many businesses now view the Arctic as some ripe new fruit, counting on global warming as the friend who will help them pick it. But ask anyone who has lived in the Arctic for a time, and they will tell you that its islands and shores are strewn with the bleached remnants of such ambition: shipping costs that mounted beyond control, inconstant yield, disastrous turns of weather. Who can count the number of disappointed ventures?

Inevitably, the next couple of decades promise the illusion of boom for the Arctic—perhaps, in some stranger brains, the mistaken belief that a warmer North is about to sprout trees, spawning its own little Toronto. That simply won't happen. Warming aside, the Arctic fails to meet many of the requirements for agriculture and construction along southern standards (scarcity of gravel being but one example). Some might resort to the argument that population is a non-factor, that fleets of international ships will directly connect North to South. But the attempt to have this very thing is what, I believe, may lay the groundwork for tragedy. My greatest fear is that shipping interests, driven by blind speculation, will brave the stew of icebergs resulting from inconstant freezing, only to spill ice-gutted bellies into Arctic waters. How long, I wonder, will Arctic communities have to suffer such disasters, before those companies finally pull out?

The Inuit, until that day, will have to be patient, adapt, just as their ancestors did the last time the planet warmed. Hopefully, my words are fantasy, and this is a deranged vision I've presented. Hopefully, Inuit will not have to stand over the wreckage of the overambitious, left in the wake of our strange era—unique only in that it is the first in which humankind has had the hubris to term the Arctic "predictable." But Inuit will adapt, no matter the outcome, even as they whisper prayers over the skeletons of those who refused to do the same. For Inuit know, of old, that the Land never fully lends itself to resource.

It is a force, and it is *nalunaktuq*.

Pijariiqpunga ("That's all I have to say").

TWO 2020 SCENARIOS

BY GEORGE ELLIOTT CLARKE

Scenario I: The Birth of Atlantica

The strangest truth about Canada, as many Americans and other observers are now recognizing in this momentous year 2020, now that the "Great White North" is dissolving, is that Canadians had always been ambivalent about their country.

And not only the French-speaking ones (whose ambivalence—or actual enmity—was most loudly articulated), but everyone: aboriginal people rightly discontented with their powerlessness and their poverty; immigrants, who often, generations after arrival and settlement, felt strong emotional and psychological ties to homelands that many had never seen; Westerners jealous of Eastern political dominance; East Coasters resentful of central Canadian financial clout; and Northerners alienated from "imperial" Ottawa and the South.

True, Canada had always been a peculiar place: a North American wilderness whose actual head-of-state was located overseas (and seldom visited); with two official languages spoken, but really unilingual (depending on geography); and the slightly weird practice of stamping, on the reverse of the monarch's face, the images of animals its heavily citified population rarely, if ever, saw.

Bizarrely, too, Canadians were always looking outside the country to Britain, France, the United States, or to China, India, or the Caribbean—for their cultural support, for a reflection of "themselves," and even for respect.

It is now clear that Canadians, in general, never had faith in the decision of their Yankee and habitant ancestors who rejected the American Revolution and set about creating, in truth, a deliberately reactionary country (even though this winter-influenced state had to accept social spending, government programs, and a national police force).

The big surprise for most outsiders is that, after Quebec voted for clear independence last year, the "Rest of Canada" so quickly splintered into regional entities too.

Of course, the rich Western provinces, whose raw resources and water are so appealing to the United States, have found it relatively easy to coalesce, setting up a government headquartered in Calgary.

Although now independent, Quebec finds it necessary to maintain a close economic and semi-political union with Ontario.

(How ironic that the originating cause of Canadian Confederation—the union of colonial Ontario and Quebec—is once again a de facto reality. They should call it "Canada II.")

Most observers of the collapse of Canada had written off the Atlantic provinces—New Brunswick, Nova Scotia, Prince Edward Island, and Newfoundland (especially after Quebec annexed Labrador as part of its settlement with Canada)—but that supposition was based on a deep ignorance of history.

Canada's first "separatists"—way back in 1867—were Nova

Scotians. Long before the Bloc Québécois ever entered Parliament, Nova Scotia returned nineteen anti-Confederation MPS in the first federal election.

During the Meech Lake Crisis in 1990 and the second Quebec Referendum in 1995, Nova Scotian leaders had mused publicly that, if Quebec left Canada, they would try to join the United States.

Many had scoffed at this suggestion back then, but now it is coming to be. And why not?

First, there are strong cultural and familial ties between New England and Atlantic Canada. No one there forgets that when Halifax, Nova Scotia, suffered, in 1917, the biggest man-made explosion before the A-bombing of Hiroshima, Japan, the first medical help on the scene came from Massachusetts.

Second, there are sound economic reasons for the formation of "Atlantica," as the new nation—and the economic union with northeastern New England and upstate New York—is to be called. Together, Atlantica and its main partners comprise some twelve million people and an economy that is, respectably, the twentieth largest on Earth.

Already, many Atlantica businesses—led by Irving Oil, McCain Foods, Sobeys, Moosehead Breweries, and the new, state-owned Atlantic Petrol—are expanding rapidly throughout New England.

At the same time, increased trade with China, India, the West Indies, and Europe is leading to record-breaking container-shipping records for the ice-free, deep-water ports of Halifax and Saint John, New Brunswick.

Also crucial to the developing success of the former East Coast of the former Canada is an expanded commitment to higher education and to immigration.

Nevertheless, these interests had always been part and parcel of Atlantica.

During Confederation, a common joke was that the greatest East Coast export was "brains." Two of Canada's big banks—the Royal Bank and the Bank of Nova Scotia—were started in Nova Scotia, a province that also boasted ten respected universities, including six in the capital, Halifax (back in 2005, Halifax's Dalhousie University's medical school outranked Harvard's, and it was the only Canadian university to crack the top-ten list).

John F. Kennedy, the thirty-fifth president of the United States, and his brother, Robert, senator for New York, both received honorary doctorates, in, respectively, 1956 and 1967, from the University of New Brunswick–Fredericton, a city whose provincial art gallery hosts a Dali.

The Atlantic provinces of Canada always were highly sophisticated in terms of post-secondary education, just as Atlantica is now.

But expanding immigration is where the incoming government is concentrating its energies.

One reason why the United States dominated the twentieth century economically and culturally is because, generally, it welcomed immigrants, especially those from Europe.

However, since 9/11 and the expansion of the non-Anglo (and non-white) population, Americans have so restricted immigration that the nation is becoming less open to innovation, experiment, and the world. Atlantica is intent on avoiding this mistake. The new government is planning to streamline acceptance of foreign accreditation of medical, engineering, and science professionals, while ensuring that newcomers are security screened enough to satisfy wary Americans.

If it succeeds, it may serve to help America once again welcome "aliens" and enjoy the benefits of their creativity and productivity (then again, for much of the last century, the first part of Canada that most immigrants saw was Halifax—even if they refused to settle there).

One far-sighted and ingenious development, tied to education and immigration, is the introduction of compulsory Chinese, Hindi, or Spanish, in Atlantica's universities. Students who graduate with one of these trade-important languages (along with, of course, English or French) enjoy the first pick of civil-service careers—that is, if they do not accept the lucrative offers of the private sector.

The primary challenge for Atlantica will be to improve communication and transportation around its constituent parts and also into the United States. If it can do that, the day may come when Quebec or other ex-Canadian provinces will be seeking to join it.

Then again, prior to Canadian Confederation, during the days of sail, Britain's Maritime colonies—Nova Scotia, Prince Edward Island, and New Brunswick—had enjoyed relatively high prosperity. They were sites of risk-taking and entrepreneurial activity.

There is every reason to expect Atlantica to restore that "Golden Age."

Scenario II: Indigenizing the Monarchy
(A Light-hearted Alternative)

Until this year, 2020, Canada had the world's most unusual monarchy, because, save for Canadian monarchists, no one gave it much thought.

Although King Charles III's visage appeared on the nation's stamps and coins, most Canadians believed they inhabited a republic—even if the head of state wore a crown and lived abroad.

Canada's very few anti-monarchists (we have never had a strong or popular republican movement) could gain no audience or hearing, for, though symbols of the monarch were plentiful, he seemed exactly that: merely a symbol, that is to say, inconsequential, almost to the point of invisibility.

Thus, most Canadians saw the monarchy as irrelevant—certainly not worth fighting over.

Moreover, they liked it; it helped distinguish us from the dangerous Yanks and their loud, bloody republic. Then, too, the "British" (actually Canadian by law) royals were a source of harmless fun (especially when they showed up in the London tabloids for one peccadillo or another).

All that changed last month during the April Crisis, when the Governor General of Canada, Conrad Blackburn, dismissed the New Democratic Party and Liberal coalition government of Prime Minister Kali Panday-Bourassa, Canada's first visible-minority and bluntly socialist leader, after she refused to bow to U.S. demands that Canada accept a "Star Wars" anti-ballistic-missile system installation on its territory.

The crisis arose because Blackburn had been ordered to take this action by the British government—speaking through King Charles III—due to its defence and economic alliance with the United States, an arrangement that is a practical reversal of the 1776 status quo.

While it cannot be credibly claimed that Blackburn was reluctant to dismiss Panday-Bourassa (his pro-U.S. and pro-right views are well known), it is doubtful he would have interfered so drastically with the program of a democratically elected government had not the king himself requested this action.

Thus, the once-invisible monarchy has become highly and offensively visible, galvanizing widespread protests and calls for its abolition.

However, I don't think that Canadians will surrender a royal heritage, nor do I think we should.

Rather, we need to indigenize—or nationalize—the monarchy, and for good reason. Currently, the monarchy is a symbol of the entrenched power of one ethnicity, or "race," and one form of religion.

Indeed, one may criticize the current Canadian monarchy for reinforcing, psychologically and culturally, the already well-established economic and political power of white Anglo-Saxon Protestants. The reality is antithetical to our efforts to construct a truly egalitarian, multiracial, multicultural, and officially bilingual democracy.

My modest proposal is that we combine the Canadian love of monarchy with the equally formidable Canadian love of lotteries.

I propose that, starting this year then every ten years hereafter, we select a new monarch and his or her immediate family by a lottery that is open to every taxpayer.

For ten years, the winning Canadian family will have the opportunity to grace our postage and coins, open Parliament, sign bills into law, open hospitals and new schools, review troops, and lend their names to military units.

Anyone with a criminal record or a history of mental illness, if he or she should win the lottery, would be disqualified from holding office (an important check that does not exist with the current monarchy).

This system would be just as open to chance—but much fairer and much more democratic—than the present one, in which our monarch arises utterly as a consequence of the good or bad marital and child-raising decisions of the House of Windsor.

Given the poor judgement of Charles III that has precipitated the April Crisis, we have a memorable example before our very eyes of how undependable Windsorite succession is for deciding the calibre of our queens and kings.

Furthermore, I think my system would do much to enhance national unity. Every child in the United States may legitimately dream of possibly becoming the president. How much better, if, in Canada, our children could legitimately dream of becoming a real king or queen, a real prince or princess!

Following its decade of service, the Canadian Royal Family would be permitted to maintain certain titles and privileges, along with a nominal pension.

This monarchy-by-official-lottery would assume many of the duties of the office of the Governor General. Those of the lieutenant-governors, who would still be appointed by the prime minister, would remain unchanged. Nevertheless, the Governor General would continue to exist in a capacity similar to that of the U.S. vice-president: as a spare authority figure to exercise the role of the Canadian monarch, should he or she become incapacitated.

Of course, all lottery winners who accept the appointment to serve as monarch would be expected to strive to become functionally, if not fluently, bilingual (if not already).

Indeed, the primary role of the Canadian monarchy, while providing political oversight of the state (without interfering in democratic governance), would be to promote the ideals of Canadian society as enshrined in the Constitution.

The idea of a "democratic monarchy" is a contradiction. But it is surely a much healthier and creative one than the Eurocentric and colonial hierarchy that the current *ancien régime* enshrines.

True, the United States might dislike having a visible monarchy on its northern border.

But American tourists will love it.

THE FUTURE OF
DEMOCRACY

BY MARK KINGWELL

THE BASIC TENET of all democratic politics is a fiction. The
tenet is that each one of us, simply by virtue of having existence thrust upon us, has a say in how our society is structured
and run—in fact, that any society not so beholden to our desire is illegitimate. Here, says Hegel, quantity becomes quality,
as if by magic. The natural fact of birth mystically acquires
the normative regard of law.

A fiction, then, because so often untrue in practice; but a
bracing one guided by searching, unfinished movement. The
vast majority of human history has run with no such belief in
play. If democracy seems basic and best to us now—to the extent that we are even willing, along with our friends to the
south and across the Atlantic, forcibly to export it—it is well to
remember that the experiment of *demos polis* is still in its infancy. Our notions about democracy date from no earlier than
about 1670, and even that is a scholarly stretch given that the
modern forms of electoral politics are essentially twentieth-
century inventions.

The reasons for qualifying our regard of democracy run
beyond its youth and potential for abuse, however. Democracy
is not just exclusive, it is frequently bizarre. Plato distrusted

the *demos* because, like many a leader today, he did not really trust the people to act in their own best interest. Desires are too strong for most people to master, he argues in *The Republic*, and a city that gave in to democracy was, he thought, ripe for domination by the clever demagogue he called the tyrant. Hence, the need for the philosopher-king, who would guarantee justice by virtue of his great wisdom (and a strict division of labour).

In a varied country like Canada, where not so long ago Don Cherry was voted the nation's leading public intellectual (I'm not making that up), such elitism is of course impossible to utter, even if it is secretly harboured. Politicians have become brokers of interest rather than leaders, and citizens reduce themselves to consumers of goods and services enjoyed in return for regular obedience to the tax code. This devolution, however efficient, does little to improve the status of politicians: a recent Angus Reid poll found that just 15 per cent of Canadians trust their elected public servants, a sad story that is, more sadly still, news to nobody. Elections, meanwhile, are stolen with impunity even in countries that claim to be in democracy's vanguard. (It helps if your brother is the governor of the disputed territory.)

The kicker is that none of the other pressing issues of our shared future—dwindling resources, climate change, global water degradation—is likely to be addressed effectively unless and until elected governments get in on the action. And they will only do that if we citizens insist on it.

THIS WILL NOT BE EASY. One clear future for democracy runs roughly as follows. Let's call it the "Dark Age Ahead," or DAA, scenario, after the bestselling gloom manual by the late Jane Jacobs.

Greater and greater distrust of the process combines with mounting cynicism among those who contest elections. Technological advances create more, rather than fewer, opportunities for electoral abuse even as the gap between tech haves and have-nots widens. Political apathy grows more widespread, fed by a popular culture of comprehensive banality and the sort of blind affluence that consumes products and services without ever asking the real cost of their availability.

The wealthy countries of the developed West grow ever fatter in their all-leisure-all-the-time manner, ignoring the growing unrest over water, food, and disease among the vast bulk of the planet's people now living in the megacities of Asia, Africa, and South America, with their vertiginous combinations of futuristic luxury for the top percentile and medieval immiseration for the rest. So much for democracy's promise at the global level. At the national level, meanwhile, democracy declines into a parody of itself, a hyper-mediated sideshow that commands dwindling interest, such that some ten times more people are moved to vote for an aspiring television singer or potential fashion model than for a leader.

Ah! you will say, that is the present, not the future. And of course you would be right. The DAA scenario is merely a modest extension of existing trends, based on the sound predictive principle that most people, and certainly most politicians, fail to change their self-harming behaviour even in the face of massive evidence—particularly if they are palliated by rounds of shopping and relentless brain-dead television.

Under these conditions, no amount of tinkering with policy levers or, still less, attempts to market politicians as if they were aspiring singers or fashion models, will do anything to lessen the damage. On the contrary, that is the political equivalent of widening freeways as a response to traffic or adding belt holes as a cure for overeating. Giving in is giving over, and heightening the media image of politics cannot ever be its salvation. It is all reminiscent of the therapeutic definition of insanity: "Doing the same things over and over and hoping for different results."

If the DAA scenario has any value, it is negative. It issues a call to action based on the perception that history, if not quite over, in the manner predicted by Hegel or Francis Fukuyama, is nevertheless stalled. Democratization, so far from ushering in a conflict-free, post-historical comfort for all, has generated new pockets of suffering, new chasms of inequality. Progress has been revealed as a dangerous addiction to technology and fossil fuels. The Western forms, moreover, perceived as licentious, are resisted, sometimes violently, by those of more transcendental conviction. The stall lies in there being no credible alternative. If not democracy, then what? If not freedom for all, then freedom for whom?

WHAT SORTS OF SHIFTS in action or structure could usher in a different democratic future: not the dark demagoguery of the Roman forum, with its bread and circuses, but the airy public space of the Athenian agora?

Well, instead of making predictions about what democracy will be like in 2020—a mere three or four elections away, after all—allow us to do something actually much more future-oriented, which is to express some rational hopes about democratic experiment. The phrase is not an oxymoron, I assure you. Though hope frequently gets a bad rap from the hard-headed, its thoughtful forms are not just rational but, to the present point, indispensable in any flourishing polity. Hope is, among other things, the most activist of citizen virtues.

We express these hopes negatively, in the form of identifying the most proximate dangers to the basic optimism of all democratic politics, together with their solutions. If democracy is to shape a bright rather than dark future, we all must act to resist the following threats, in ascending order of seriousness:

1. *Reductive populism.* We regularly decry the elitism and arrogance of our elected leaders, but the alternatives usually offered—direct democracy, regular plebiscites, vote by numbers—are afflicted by the same youngest-common-denominator pathology that reduces so much cultural production to the sophistication level of a twelve-year-old. In our version of the "here comes everybody" syndrome, we get, not the vaunted "hive mind" or so-called "wisdom of crowds," but just a reduction of everything to aggregated passing desire. Crowds can be dumb as well as wise. Resting political decision making on them is

the political equivalent of solving the ills of big media by giving everyone a blog.

Solution: more proportional representation, but not at the expense of parliamentary supremacy. The virtue of electoral politics, when they work, is to find the optimum distance between majoritarian muscle and elite domination. Elected governments and a separation of powers are essential to this balance (though see the next point on why we need more decentralization).

2.Bureaucratization and its evil twin, cynicism. Democracy has been facetiously defined as the freedom to choose who will get the blame, but bureaucracy—rule by no one—ensures that there is no one to blame. Thus the standard democratic fear of experts or elites is actually far outstripped by the danger of institutional nonentities. The familiar "tragedy of the commons"—whereby what is owned by none is neglected by all—is now made into governmental infrastructure. The resulting who-cares attitude by neglected citizens is more than just media-saturated malaise; it is the rational response of agents who feel nobody is accountable, hence that demands of accountability are a sucker bet.

Solution: increased civic participation. Calls for democratic participation are common, but they too often succumb to what democratic theorist Carole Pateman called "solely protective participation"; that is, the scant action of helping to decide who the decision makers will be. Decentralization of governance, not only practicable but necessary in complex societies, is the only way citizens will remain connected to the effects of political decision making. It is too easy to disavow unjust policy when it is made opaque and distant.

3.Exclusive claims. By far the gravest clear danger to the future of democracy is the creeping loss of its rational centre: The idea, best defended by the German philosopher Jürgen Habermas, that "the unforced force of the better argument" is the basis of social justice. That is another way of saying that, in the public sphere, discursive reason is the one and only standard by which democratic arrangements can be assessed. Truth is not assumed; indeed, truth is not the regulative ideal of democracy, justice is. Public argument is always "futural": We strive to come closer, to get better, to refine.

The threat posed by exclusive claims is twofold: obvious external enemies, who regard liberal reason as the satanic enemy; and less obvious internal enemies, including both identity politicians and presidents, who rely on inner conviction rather than public argument. Any political position that claims access to god's will, the spirit of the people, or the impossible-to-share experience of oppression is inherently anti-democratic. It assumes a purity of conclusion or community that is foreign to the experiment. Democracy can, indeed must, embrace criticism and otherness; that is its genius. Assertions of privileged knowledge or essential truth are not criticism, however; they are ideology.

Solution: citizen education understood as cultivation of public reason. In ancient societies, all educated people were versed in rhetoric, the art of rational persuasion. Nowadays "rhetoric" is just another word for "spin." All citizens need to be initiated by schools and universities in the discipline of making good arguments and criticizing bad ones. And politicians need to lead by example. Logic for everyone!

4.*Comfort*. The only reason this danger ranks higher as a threat to democratic hope than the previous ones is because it is so stealthy and hard to resist. It is the enemy we cannot fight because we cannot see.

We in Canada often appear to believe, say while contesting a federal election or, still more, viewing a leaders' debate, that the larger, world-historical tectonics of democratic threats are not our concern. Our worries rise and fall with the state of the GST, disbursement of transfer payments, softwood lumber tariffs, maybe border security. The great fiction of Canadian democracy—a fiction more pernicious than the systemic one at every democracy's heart—is that our polity can continue on more or less its present course no matter what happens elsewhere. Canadian society, whatever its own intramural inequalities and injustices, is a privileged bubble that floats above a roiling cauldron of human desire and need.

Solution: public spaces and public debates that centre on the transnational obligations of all democrats.

THERE IS A PECULIAR BENEFIT to our bubble, and here hope enters the picture in positive guise. Canadians enjoy, at their best and most responsible, a political perspective denied, per circumstance, to others. This perspective is not a matter of our much celebrated multiculturalism—in practice, more a matter of rival World Cup flags than anything substantive. It is, instead, a function of Canada's status as a postmodern democracy in a world struggling with pre-modern misery and modern domination. Across an unlikely land mass, a varied and shifting populace strives to achieve not simply a hands-off modus vivendi but an ongoing discursive enactment of justice.

The achievement could be an example to the world, but only if we take the world into account. Canadians (including other writers in this volume) often lament their loss of a place in global affairs, but they rarely consider the loss of the globe's place with them. Justice doesn't stop at the border, and neither does democracy, even if sovereignty and citizenship do. Exporting democracy is democracy's inner logic: It is, and always has been, a matter of extending the given. How we assert ourselves outside our borders will determine whether Canada continues to deserve the title of democratic nation. The "gift of democracy" is a phrase with a double-genitive meaning, the "of" running significant, and reinforcing, meanings in both directions. That is: giving democracy, but also what democracy gives.

The old rap against democracy was that it encouraged levelling: of class distinctions, of course, but perhaps also of excellence, resulting in a state-wide version of the tall-poppy syndrome. In the words of Gilbert and Sullivan, "if everybody's somebody, nobody's anybody." The new challenge for democrats is not that one, which is much exaggerated. No, the real challenge for Canadian democrats is, rather, to continue extending and extending the promise of justice for everyone— which is likewise justice, indeed life, for ourselves.

Until everybody's somebody, nobody's anybody.

CANADA SANS QUEBEC:
THE FIFTY-FIRST STATE

BY CHANTAL HÉBERT

THE EYES OF THE WORLD are on the former Canadian federation on this first Tuesday of November, 2020 as its nineteen million voters participate for the first time in an American presidential election as full-fledged U.S. citizens.

The outcome of one of the most closely fought election battles in recent American history will be a close one. It is expected that the fifty new Electors from Canada will ultimately tip the balance in favour of one of the two women who are vying for the presidency.

On this voting day, the American public is more deeply divided as to the future course of their nation than it has been in decades. Voters are torn between the militarist approach privileged by the successive Republican administrations that have occupied the White House without interruption since the early days of the twenty-first century, and the Democrat promise to restore multilateralism and move to a more open peace economy.

Since the withdrawal of the United States from the main international forums ten years ago and the subsequent relocation of the United Nations outside American soil, it is the first time a serious presidential candidate campaigns on the promise to re-engage the country in formal international dialogue.

In the interval, the Republican administration has gone to extraordinary lengths to keep the country safe from terrorist attacks. The result has been a full decade free of such deadly incidents, at least on American soil, but also a physical and political isolation on par with that of the Soviet Bloc of the previous century.

The central role that the traditionally progressive Canadian voters could play in the outcome of this pivotal election is exactly what the best minds in the international community had hoped for when they originally rallied behind the plan to have the former federation become an American state.

A decade ago, most of the big players on the international scene supported a radical redrawing of the North American political map as part of a last-ditch effort to try to change the balance between isolationists and multilateralists from within the last remaining military superpower.

The stakes involved in this battle by proxy between the American right and much of the progressive forces of the democratic world are unprecedented. Inspired by the American resolve to stay out of all multilateral forums and framework agreements, China and India have gone down the path of a no-holds-barred practice of capitalism, making giant economic leaps but at huge costs to the global environment and to the financial health of poorer nation-states. Short of a dramatic shift in U.S. policy, the trend to a world that puts the leading-edge technology at the service of feudal values will be irreversible.

The morphing of Canada into a political Trojan Horse,

invested with the best last hopes of much of the planet's progressive forces, did not take place overnight or easily. Without the irresistible pressures of the international community and the many calls to the social conscience of Canadians, the project to join the American political union would never have rallied the 66 per cent support required to pass the test of the 2010 referendum.

Pushed to the brink by the virtual closure of the Canada-U.S. border in the wake of the 2008 terrorists attacks and the partial destruction of three of that country's major cities, corporate Canada lined up early and to a man and a woman behind an urgent redefinition of Canada's political status. On Wall Street and among corporate America's political allies in the White House, the notion of making Canada a formal part of the United States had traction from the very start.

After 2001, the acquisition by the U.S. of energy reserves sheltered from the ideological currents that regularly sweep the planet in reaction or in opposition to the latest American doctrine became a strategic priority. Hundreds of thousands of American troops fanned out to distant fronts in the name of keeping America and its economy safe. But on this ever-changing front, the very notion of what would amount to a decisive victory became elusive. By 2010, a battle-weary American public was more than open to a political change that would allow the U.S. to make strides towards the goal of energy security by peaceful means.

Yet, without the stunning decision of the alter-globalization movement, and in particular its influential environmental wing, to forcefully support Canada's entry into the United

States, the project would likely never have seen the light of day. On both sides of the Canada-U.S. border, and from the main capitals of the rest of the world, some of the most influential progressive voices on the planet joined with those of the corporate right to urge Canada to become part of the United States in an attempt to redeem the planet from inside America.

Quebec also threw its weight behind the project once Washington and Ottawa agreed to offer the former province the status of associate state with the new political entity. By so doing, the two governments fulfilled a key requirement of La Francophonie, the international club of French-speaking countries. Their support for the merger had been conditional on the maintenance of a politically autonomous French-language society in North America.

As opposed to the citizens of its former sister provinces, Quebecers therefore did not fully adhere to the American political union. While Quebec has a first-row seat on today's pivotal presidential election, its people are nevertheless only spectators of the suspense taking place next door.

In exchange for its political autonomy, Quebec is also bound to conduct its foreign policy on the basis of strict neutrality. It has agreed to deploy its armed forces abroad only as part of peacekeeping missions. Over the past five years, Quebec troops have become a presence in many regions of Africa, a continent that continues to be neglected by an international community obsessed with the absence of the United States from its ranks.

Besides a framework trade agreement giving it conditional access to the American markets, Quebec has also been granted most of the powers that the former national state of Canada still exercised at the time it joined the U.S. By then, they did not amount to much. Canada had already given up control over its airspace and its ports after the United States unilaterally took over its northern partner's defence, once an investigation revealed that the 2008 terrorist attacks had been masterminded by a cell operating out of St. John's, Newfoundland.

Under its last Liberal government, Canada adopted the U.S. dollar in a last-ditch effort to breathe life into a domestic economy strangled by the many physical and virtual controls put in place by its powerful neighbour for security purposes. The two countries had also agreed on a joint immigration policy, and a common ID card had been issued to their citizens.

The day-to-day governance of Quebec did not change dramatically under its new political status, but its social and linguistic makeup have been substantially altered. In exchange for a two-year open-door policy between the soon-to-be defunct rest of Canada and Quebec, the latter's share of the Canadian debt was wiped off the books.

Close to four million Canadians from the other provinces took advantage of the grace period agreed upon by their governments to relocate in Quebec, thus increasing its population by 50 per cent almost overnight.

The massive arrival of so many newcomers—most of them fully bilingual but almost all of them devoid of francophone roots—has altered Quebec's political makeup in ways that the negotiators of the open-doors agreement had not foreseen.

Drawn by the prospect of maintaining the former Canadian social model, many former charter members of Canada's progressive establishment elected to live out their days in Quebec rather than die as American citizens. Three former leaders of the defunct federal NDP, the entire parliamentary caucus of the federal Green Party, an octogenarian ex-leader of the former Progressive Conservative Party of Canada, as well as the last two premiers of Ontario all elected to move to Quebec. The latter two opted to relocate after they lost the battle to turn Ontario into a state distinct from Canada in the wake of the decision to make Calgary the capital of the new American state.

Besides changing the language mix, the transition from province of a defunct federation to associate state of the U.S. has profoundly modified Quebec's political landscape. Mario Dumont, who served as the first president of the new Quebec, could also have been its last native-born head of state for a long time. Too far to the right for the new critical mass of progressive voters that resulted from the resettlement of so many other Canadians, Dumont's reign did not survive the changed political demography of Quebec.

Devoid of its historical raison d'être, the Parti Québécois reinvented itself as a centrist and nationalist party along the lines of the former Liberal Party of Canada. Under its reconfigured shape, the former sovereignist party expanded into many new constituencies, in particular the new Quebecers from the rest of Canada who used to admire some of the sovereignist leaders from afar and with decidedly mixed feelings in the old days of the twentieth-century sovereignist-federalist debate.

As a result, the 2017 Quebec presidential election saw the

advent of a Saskatchewan-born Péquiste head of state whose first language is English. That election also featured a challenger issued from a brand new party, Canadian Party of Quebec (CPQ), committed to having Quebec join its former Canadian partner as an American state.

Promoters of this new party are essentially francophone and progressive. They feel that the coming together of Canada and Quebec under a single American roof would allow the latter to leave its marginal status behind and become a full-fledged player on the most important political checkerboard on the planet.

They argue that Quebec, as an associate state operating apart from the United States, will never truly be able to have its voice heard in the concert of nations. Instead, its citizens will be relegated to second-class status under the emerging world order. The notion of making alliances with the former Canada so as to increase the progressive influence of both on the rest of America is also central to the goals of the new party.

Finally, some defenders of the French language feel that it would be easier to maintain a French-speaking environment in Quebec if its anglophone elements had a chance to fan out across the United States, rather than have their horizons limited to the former province.

In 2017, the party had a marginal impact on the outcome of the vote. It hit a wall in the regions where the new Quebecers, who came to the province because of its distinct political status, have settled. By and large, the newer anglophone and allophone communities are determined to preserve and protect the autonomy of their elected port of call.

But today's American presidential vote could have a huge impact on the Quebec debate. If the U.S., under the impetus of progressive Canadian voters, reconciles itself with multilateralism on the international stage, the result would provide a major boost to those in Quebec who promote a reunion with the former Canadian federation. They could also bank on a more sympathetic hearing at the White House and count on a more open attitude to language accommodations.

The advent of dramatically different American dynamics as a result of today's vote could turn the new CPQ into a serious player in the elections that are slated to take place in the former province next year. If it comes to power, the CPQ is committed to holding a referendum on Quebec accession to full American statehood, alongside the former Canada, before the end of its first mandate.

As opposed to the 2010 Canadian referendum, but in line with Quebec tradition, a simple majority would suffice to trigger the negotiations that would lead to the extinguishing of Quebec's so recently acquired special status.

BOOMERS IN AN IDEOLOGICAL, POLITICAL, AND ENVIRONMENTAL CAULDRON

BY DAVID WALKER

MARY AWOKE TO FIND her breathing to be much easier, no doubt due to the recent reprogramming of her implanted nanomed dispenser. Despite the rather nasty political issues surrounding the new technology, it was certainly light years ahead of the way in which chronic diseases were managed even a decade or two ago, and Mary was grateful she qualified for it.

Simple really, when you think about it, and not very different from the technology that kept her fridge stocked and her air quality monitored. Minute monitoring chips were now contained in most products and appliances. Her food program monitored consumption and fridge inventory, communicating directly with the food supplier, who restocked on a regular basis. Shopping, when not done electronically, was simpler when not requiring checkout; a device assessed prices as you walked out of the store and deducted same from the bank account identified by your unique identifier, often implanted in your wrist.

As it applied to medical care, rather than visiting a doctor or a lab for tests, waiting for results, and receiving prescribed medication, thanks to developments in nanotechnology and software innovation, an array of measurements of bodily function were taken by minuscule implanted chips. Mary's biometrics were silently and invisibly computed in real time, and her nanomed simply created and infused the correct medication to adjust the various functions required. Activity profiles were also transmitted to the bio-engineering section of her disease-management unit, and occasional reprogramming was undertaken without the need for frequent personal interaction.

Changes in what used to be called "health care" in the developed world had been profound. An aging population that demanded constant fine-tuning, allied with extremely expensive innovations and interventions, had required a significant overhaul of the system. The realization that, organized as it was, the system could not meet demand was a seminal moment in public-policy development, and the now infamous Kingston Conference of 2009 had identified the precepts and constructs of a new approach. These worthy principles and the changes that followed had only recently been usurped by significant socio-political action.

However, in the decade following 2009, building on earlier reforms to primary care, multi-disciplinary alternatives to physician-based care had been amplified. Physician assistants, nurse practitioners, and other providers had joined doctors and nurses in large teams, which were responsible for the care of defined populations and were required to meet multiple defined-performance standards. Health metrics of individuals and the target population were constantly monitored and related to the standards prescribed. Funding and reimbursement were tightly linked to outcomes and health status, not to items of process, such as visits or procedures.

What had been hospital-based care was also radically altered, with similar substitutions to skill activities such as anesthesia, pain management, endoscopy, and a variety of interventional and surgical procedures. Many of these procedures were now done in low-cost environments, often in the primary-care setting, and hospitals were reserved for complex, high-risk, multidisciplinary activities.

One of the Kingston Conference principles addressed the woeful lack of information systems and management in the system as it was, and a combination of massive public and private investment in information technology was undertaken. Over two years, the system truly became measurable and, to a far greater extent, intelligent. The investment in IT allowed a true picture to be taken of needs, capacity, productivity, effectiveness, and quality. Its effect was profound.

It became immediately apparent that the system in place was incredibly inefficient. Mary recalled the passage through the system of her father, Bill, who, at the age of seventy-five, developed a sore hip and a limp. He visited his elderly physician, who practised alone, although it took some weeks to see the doctor, who worked only part-time. Bill was given a requisition for an X-ray, but lost it and had to return for a replacement. He visited a radiology facility for the X-ray, and then waited for his next appointment to hear that it showed some hip arthritis, and that a CT scan had been recommended. The GP ordered the scan and, after another visit, he decided that he required a consultant's opinion.

The GP's favourite orthopedic surgeon, his golf partner, had a long waiting list to be seen, but Bill was reassured he was the best and worth waiting for. Months elapsed during which he suffered considerable disability, becoming unable to maintain his attempts at fitness by walking and swimming. He eventually saw the surgeon, who told him he needed an operation and new hip, but that he should be assessed for fitness to withstand surgery first. Puzzled that this hadn't been done during the interminable wait to see the surgeon, Bill revisited the GP, who arranged for him to see an internist, whom he saw some weeks later. A concerning electrocardiogram prompted a rather quicker transit to a cardiologist, who performed a stress test, which, not surprisingly, was negative. Armed with papers and reports, Bill went back to the surgeon, who felt it was now time to proceed and placed Bill's name on the waiting list. Some months passed, and Bill was twice given dates for surgery. On each occasion he arranged for Mary to take time off work to help him, but on both occasions his surgery was "bumped" due to unanticipated trauma workloads and a shortage of nurses. When Bill was finally called in, the hospital had neither a record of his preadmission work-up nor his history, and most of it had to be repeated, since his internist and cardiologist were both away on holiday and the information could not be accessed.

The surgery was eventually performed, successfully, and Bill began a long path of rehabilitation, made necessary by the two-year degradation in strength and fitness caused by his disability.

The advent of sophisticated IT allowed inefficiencies in the system to be identified and new protocols developed. Mary noted that, five years later, when her father's other hip began to cause trouble, he was already being monitored by his primary-care team, in part driven by prompts from his Web-based electronic medical record. A scan was booked immediately, performed at the same time as his visit, in the same building, and he was seen that same day by the orthopedic nurse-specialist, who was in direct email contact with the orthopedic surgical team, the CT scan being attached to the email for easy viewing, just as it was available on his secure online record. The decision was taken to replace the hip, but with new technology this was to be a much simpler procedure. The clinic's nurse-practitioner provided Web access regarding Bill's health status information to the surgical team, and the following week, Bill had the procedure done under local anesthesia, delivered by an anesthesia technician, while the surgery was performed by the most available surgeon in the group in a facility protected from the unpredictable effects of trauma and human-resource shortages. Bill walked out of the surgi-clinic later that night to begin rehab, delivered in his home by the physio team that was an integral part of his primary-care team.

It had seemed that disease-management reform was well under way in the early teens of the century, but stumbling economies, environmental change, continued global unrest, and political instability had led to erosion in universal access, measurable and achievable standards, and reasonable cost control.

In Mary's case, like that of so many others, serious lung disease had developed quite quickly in recent years as air quality plummeted. A combination of factors had allowed remarkable global warming, which followed an exponential and uncontrolled path, accelerating far more quickly than predicted. Those who had claimed that the early warning signs were simply part of natural variation had become silent in recent years. This, combined with the continued use of carbon fuels for industry, transportation, and—more critical for the average person—cooling, had led to a hotter, dirtier, world.

The political and personal fallout from these developments worried and saddened Mary. Ideological and religious conflict had rippled out from the disasters of the early part of the century. Who would have guessed that 9/11 marked the beginning of an unending war, one that had seen the remarkable moving of the state of Israel from the Middle East to what once was Panama, and the ascension to power in much of the world of fundamentalist and extremist governments.

Such persistent conflict had led to new alliances; much of Europe now identified itself with the Muslim states of the Middle East, mostly on the basis of continued socio-cultural demographic change and the need to access oil-based energy sources. China, Russia, and Japan formed an impressive socio-political block, leaving the now united Americas defending poor isolated Britain and Australasia.

Such ongoing conflict precluded any possibility of progress in addressing issues of global importance, such as the environment or the ever-diverging standards of health, and the recent demise of the United Nations and World Health Organizations worried Mary and her friends.

Mary's worries were more personal as well. At home, a major intergenerational political divide had marked the past decade, created by the powerful influence of her generation, once known as baby boomers. Now in their sixties and seventies, this enormous demographic cohort continued to leave an enormous footprint on society. Shortly after the United States of All-America was formed (All America!), a new party, the Progressive Elder Party, came into existence with the sole platform of addressing the needs of elders, and it was rapidly elected to power. Legislation protecting the rights of elders in access to new health and social services had alienated the generations that followed, including Mary's children and grandchildren. Heavily taxed, they resented the cohort-centric public policies of the elders. The first indication of such selfishness had been the abandonment of mandatory retirement, allowing this wealthy generation to remain attached to well-paying senior jobs at the expense of the progress of their natural successors. The second was differential access to health care for elders, a public policy that ensured the PE party would continue to be elected, despite the internecine feuds it generated.

Despite missing her family, Mary enjoyed the senior compound in which she lived with her lifelong friends, playing cards, listening to music, and watching movies from her youth. She missed her golf, but lack of water and the heat had ruined golf courses. In any event, despite her nanomed, bad air and her breathing precluded more than minimal exercise.

Scanning one of the wall-screens in her unit for a report on her biometrics, Mary was heartened to see on the CNN mini-screen that the anticipated exhaustion of world oil supplies was actually beginning to have an effect on global politics. An unlikely alliance of scientists from China and All-America had continued work on alternative nuclear and hydrogen-based energy systems, and it seemed possible that they could be applied quite rapidly. There also had been substantial theoretical progress on carbon-based gas expulsion from the atmosphere, and small-scale experiments over Antarctica had been successful, although the resultant cooling of the local atmosphere there had interrupted the hunting that had developed since the ice cap melted. Plans were afoot to undertake larger trials, with the anticipated effect of global cooling and conversion to alternative energy sources. These developments pleased Mary, as she did not wish to see her grandchildren inherit the inhospitable world her generation had created.

Mary was also realistic enough to foresee the end of the influence of her generation; its numbers and resultant power were already waning, as the fortunes of the undertakers flourished. Cremation was mandatory and ash-scattering the norm, cemeteries having been converted to somewhat arid public parkland some years ago. A coalition of political parties were proposing massive tax advantages and social support for child-bearing and, in anticipation of the demise of the PE government, Mary's grandchildren's generation were producing children at the rate of five per family. Demographers were identifying a baby boom and predicted that it would have a defining effect on society.

IGNORING THE CANARIES

BY DAVID SUZUKI

BACK IN THE YEAR 2006, a trip to a hospital emergency room anywhere in the world when a smog alert was issued was a revelation. The rooms were packed with children and the elderly suffering from severe asthmatic attacks. Medical staff were scurrying to handle the case overload, as adults anxiously brought their elderly parents or their young children to the hospital.

Looking back from the vantage point of 2020, the scene should have dispelled any doubts that our health was directly related to the quality of our environment.

Like canaries in a coal mine, whose hypersensitivity to deadly sour gas gave miners an early warning to get out of the pits, the asthmatic children and the aged were informing us in 2006 that we had poisoned the very air that our health and well-being rely on.

When a canary keeled over, miners did not debate about how serious a threat was—they got out as fast as they could. But where was the appropriate urgent response when emergency wards were routinely jammed during pollution-filled days just fourteen or fifteen years ago and when 12 per cent of Canadian children had asthma?

Today, in 2020, we are witnessing the impact of our indifference and inaction, with millions more children and elderly needlessly dying from environmentally induced illness, with our air so polluted that "smog days" are not unusual but the norm, with our water supplies so tainted that Canada is spending billions to divert rivers that flow to the Arctic and to install water-purification systems so that even those in the cities can enjoy an occasional drink of clean water.

How did this happen? How could Canadians, and others around the world, have been so oblivious to the warning signs in 2006 that we now find ourselves on the edge of a true worldwide environmental disaster?

Perhaps an explanation of the lack of urgency is the fact that many of the patients in crisis were brought to emergency wards by loved ones driving sports utility vehicles. Clearly, the drivers had not connected the medical crisis with the way they were living, so love and concern for parents and children failed to evoke a demand to diminish the air pollution that induced the respiratory episodes.

And air quality was only one of a number of environmental problems scientists had warned of ever since Rachel Carson triggered the environmental movement in 1962 with *Silent Spring*, the book that documented the unexpected effects of pesticides. By 2006, species extinction, habitat destruction, toxic pollution of air, water, and soil, depletion of marine fishes, desertification, ozone depletion, and global warming had become part of the familiar litany of ecological problems.

If we are now to understand the nature of the issues and the solution, we have to consider our evolutionary history, which began in the savannahs of Africa some 150,000 years ago.

We appeared when mammoths, sabre-toothed tigers, giant

sloths, and moa birds still flourished on the planet. The small clusters of upright, furless apes that were our ancestors must have been an unprepossessing presence on the plains. Moving among vast herds of herbivores and predatory carnivores, those early humans gave little hint of their incredible destiny in a mere 150 millennia. We lacked impressive numbers, size, speed, strength, or sensory acuity, but our behaviour revealed our key evolutionary advantage: intelligence.

Locked inside our skulls, the two-kilogram human brain endowed us with a massive memory, insatiable curiosity, and impressive creativity, key elements for our success. The human brain invented a radical concept: the future. We know what's going on around us through our senses, but because that brain created the notion of a future, we found we could influence the future through deliberate choice made in the present.

Thus, confronted with a fork in a path, those early people might recall dangerous animals along the branch to the right while the trail to the left led to a patch of edible fruit. So, they went left. Foresight, looking ahead and recognizing opportunities while anticipating dangers, enabled us to navigate deliberately into the future. That was our strategy for survival and it was enormously successful.

In evolutionary terms, our species is in its early infancy, yet we have already become the most numerous mammal on the planet. But unlike any other mammal, our impact on our surroundings is now greatly amplified by enormous technological power that is applied on our behalf for food, clothing, shelter, communication, transportation, and so on. Over the past century, we have also become afflicted with a powerful demand for consumer goods that are supplied by a global economy that exploits the entire planet as a source of raw materials and as a place to scatter its wastes.

Thus, our numbers, technology, consumption, and global economy have made us a new kind of force that I call a "superspecies." Never before in the 3.8 billion years of life's existence, has a single species been able to alter the physical, chemical, and biological makeup of the planet on the scale of human activity today.

It has happened suddenly. For most of human existence, we were a local, tribal animal. We didn't worry about people on the other side of a mountain, desert, or ocean, but now we have to consider the collective impact of all human beings on Earth, and that's not easy. But, as we should have known in 2006, we are charting new territory. It is agonizingly cumbersome and slow. We have never had to do this before, but now we have no choice, because we have become a potent force with enormous influence on the planet and the future.

In 2006, we had all the increased capacity to look ahead through scientists, engineers, computers, and telecommunications. For more than forty years, leading scientists in the world had been warning us that we were following a dangerous path. Carson's message warned that, while scientists study nature in bits and pieces in laboratory test tubes and growth chambers, those fragments do not mimic nature. They are artefacts, devoid of context that gives them meaning, removed from the rhythms, cycles, and patterns that enable us to anticipate the consequences of our manipulations.

After Carson's book, scientists began to inform us that

humankind was exploiting the biosphere far beyond levels that could be sustained indefinitely. We were depleting nature's services upon which we remain utterly dependent—cleansing and replenishing soil and water, modulating the atmosphere, pollinating flowering plants, capturing the energy of the sun. That's why, in November 1992, leading scientists of the world, including more than half of all living Nobel laureates, signed the "World Scientists' Warning to Humanity." Here is part of what they said:

"Human beings and the natural world are on a collision course. Human activities inflict harsh and often irreversible damage on the environment and on critical resources. If not checked, many of our current practices put at serious risk the future we wish for human society ... and may so alter the living world that it will be unable to sustain life in the manner that we know. Fundamental changes are urgent if we are to avoid the collision the present course will bring about."

The document goes on to cite the primary areas of concern, including the atmosphere, oceans, water resources, soil, forests, species extinction, and population. Then, their words grow even bleaker:

"No more than one or a few decades remain before the chance to avert the threats we now confront will be lost and the prospects for humanity immeasurably diminished. We the undersigned, senior members of the world's scientific community, hereby warn all humanity of what lies ahead. A great change in our stewardship of the Earth and life on it is required if vast human misery is to be avoided and our global home on this planet is not to be irretrievably mutilated."

Scientists of such eminence do not as a rule issue such urgent and frightening statements. The response of the global media, however, was terrifying—there was virtually none. Most television and print media tended to dismiss the press release as "not newsworthy." Half of all living Nobel Prize winners suggesting that humanity could have as little as ten years to avoid an absolute catastrophe is rated unworthy of reportage by media that obsessed for weeks and months, sometimes years, over O. J. Simpson, Bill Clinton and Monica Lewinsky, Princess Diana, Michael Jackson, Martha Stewart, and Jennifer-Brad-Angelina! Now, that was frightening.

We turned our backs on the very means whereby we achieved our position on the planet: looking ahead, recognizing the dangers, searching for opportunities, and choosing the best path to survival.

But we had excuses like "the economy" and "political realities" that trumped the pronouncements of scientists. Indeed, the late George W. Bush, who was president of the United States at that time, is said to have retorted that dire warnings about climate change were simply the "opinion of scientists." We now have learned the cost of ignoring the repeated warnings of scientists on the catastrophic threats that hurricanes posed to New Orleans when Katrina hit.

If we do not use the best scientific evidence and conclusions, then politics, economics, even religions become the alternative.

How Have We Come to This Moment?

The great French molecular biologist and Nobel Prize winner, François Jacob, believes "the human brain is hard-wired for order." We find chaos or disorder frightening and attempt to create order to have a semblance of understanding the great forces impinging on our lives. In world views of every society in the past, it was understood that people are deeply embedded in and utterly dependent on the natural world in which everything is connected to everything else. In such a world, any deliberate action has repercussions and therefore is laden with responsibility.

Even today, if we listen to the stories, songs, and prayers of aboriginal and traditional people, we learn who they are and where they belong on Earth; they celebrate being part of nature and thank their Creator for nature's generosity and abundance; they acknowledge that, as part of nature, they have responsibilities, and promise over and over to act properly to keep it all going.

But for most people today, that sense of connectedness and responsibility has been lost. A number of factors have shattered our perception of the world into a mosaic of disconnected bits and pieces:

Population. As population rises rapidly, more and more people are younger and average age decreases. Most people alive today have spent their entire lives in an unprecedented and unsustainable period of growth and change, but since that's all they've ever known, it is what they think is normal and must be perpetuated.

Information explosion. The media shatter the world into bits and pieces, visual and audio bytes that are increasingly devoid of context to explain why it is important, how it came about, and what can be done about it. Stories about hurricanes, floods, drought, and forest fires are reported as if they are separate, independent events, thereby ignoring possible underlying commonalities, such as climate.

Move to cities. In the twentieth century, humankind underwent a remarkable transition from rural, village communities to big cities, where it became easy to accept the notion that human beings are different from other life forms; our intelligence has enabled us to escape the constraints of our biology and nature. We seem to create our own urban habitat where the economy delivers the services of food, electricity, water, and the disposal of garbage and sewage, when in reality, they are all made possible by the biosphere.

Global economy. Our highest priority now seems to be to ensure the continued growth of an economic system that exploits the entire planet for its vast repertoire of raw materials, while depositing our toxic wastes. The diversity of local ecosystems and communities is obliterated under the relentless drive to provide consumer goods to a global population of nine billion potential customers.

Now, in 2020, time is running out for us to put our world back together.

The challenge of our time is to recognize that we still live within the confines of a finite biosphere, the zone of air, water, and land where life exists. Our very survival and well-being are directly related to the quality of the air, water, soil, sunlight, and biodiversity around us. In this world, as for our ancestors, everything we do has repercussions and, therefore, responsibilities. We buy clothing made of cotton, leather, wool, or rubber, consumer items like cars, television sets, or computers containing metal and plastics, and food shipped from all parts of the planet, and each purchase has consequences that reverberate around the world.

What Can We Do?

Global ecological degradation results from our belief that we are different from the rest of creation, that our intelligence enables us to escape the bounds of instinct and nature so that we create our own habitat and live under the demands imposed by economics. But we forget our biological nature at our peril. Like all other life forms, we need clean air, water, soil, and energy, and biodiversity, so their protection should be our highest priority.

Is a sustainable future possible? The answer "no" to that question would be devastating. We have to answer, "It has to be."

A good exercise to begin with would be to reflect on why we live where we do, what are the values that make it a place we want our children to grow up in. And then ask where we are going.

What kind of a Canada or community would we like to see in a generation, while protecting those values? How about a country where the air is clean and fewer children come down with asthma, where we can drink the water from any river or lake, where we can catch a fish and eat it without worrying about what might be in it?

If the questions are posed that way, everyone agrees. That means we will no longer be fighting over how to improve our environment and we will have a target to guide all of our decisions.

Such a sustainable future can be achieved within a generation, in less than twenty years from today. We have to define concrete targets and timelines to reach them from year one on. We can achieve it if we get started right away.

THE REPUBLIC OF NORTHERN AMERICA

BY STÉPHANE KELLY

IN 1891, the intellectual Goldwin Smith caused a furor when he published *Canada and the Canadian Question*. He suggested that, if Canadians believed in the democratic ideal, they must accept the inevitable: annexation of Canada by the American republic.

The writer noted that the divide created by the English Civil War, which pitted Puritans against Cavaliers, had replicated itself in North America. Canadians embraced the aristocratic ideal of the Cavaliers, while Americans held dear the democratic ideal of the Puritans.

Who would have thought that roles would have reversed themselves a century later? That the United States would be seen as a society with an affinity for aristocratic values, while Canada would be perceived as an alternative model, because of its attachment to democratic values?

This reversal could change the political landscape of North America.

American society's slide towards the aristocratic ideal risks exacerbating the anger of the northern states, and possibly convincing them to leave the union.

In this context, among the political possibilities that face Canadians in 2020, it would not be far-fetched to include political integration with New England.

But before looking at how events and trends could make this possible, let's try to understand why the South and the North have become like two different nations.

FOR A LONG TIME, the northern states have been irritated by the attitude of the South. For a large portion of American history, these two regions have quarrelled. Wily and glib, southern politicians have often succeeded in manipulating Washington.

Certainly, the North succeeded at times in blocking them. But the latest southern offensive, begun in the last third of the twentieth century, is without precedent. It is taking away almost all hope that northern electors have of living according to the ideals of the founding fathers.

Economically, the South and the North are almost exact opposites. Based on natural resource exports, the economy of the South is characterized by ridiculous wages, minimal taxation, and indifference toward technological innovation and ecological balance.

With their social-democratic leanings, northern Americans reject these parameters. Their economic philosophy has remained true to the idea of the New Deal. However, in the eyes of several southern conservative politicians, it makes perfect sense to compare President Franklin D. Roosevelt to Russia's Joseph Stalin.

Another front upon which these two regions are divided is religion. The influence of evangelical Protestantism on the South alienates it from the religious sensitivities of the North.

From the beginning of the twentieth century, Protestants have become less of a force in the North, where Catholic and Jewish faiths have grown markedly. The growing pluralism of this region has marginalized religion in the political culture.

In the South, the weakness of other religions has allowed the Anglo-Saxon majority to closely associate the American way of life with evangelical Protestantism.

Hostile toward any socially progressive reform, this vision reinforces the aristocratic vision of southern society.

The North and the South also have opposing philosophies with regards to security and defence.

Southerners espouse a martial ethic, which uses repression to deal with criminality, believes in the freedom to carry weapons, and embraces an imperial attitude about national defence.

The historical evolution of the United States could have been moulded by an erasure of the division between the South and the North. Development of other regions, such as the Pacific, could have established a better balance. But this was not the case.

Perhaps societies like taking on social projects to better organize their development. But their real evolution is often subject to other factors. In fact, the North and the South have remained victims of their old demons. When the next cataclysm occurs, there will be no Lincoln to stop the bleeding.

IF THE ANNEXATIONIST VISION is imaginable, it is because there is a good historical ground for it to thrive upon. And we have underestimated this ground for a long time. We wrongly thought Canadians had always been anti-American.

After the Revolution of 1776, the elite of the Loyalist colonial towns of New England changed their point of view on the matter. In Canadian towns, people started distinguishing between bad Americans (southerners) and good Americans (northerners). These Canadians criticized southern politics, subjugated as they were by the radical republicanism of the Democratic Party under Jefferson and Madison (allied with Revolutionary France). Northern Americans were judged acceptable because of their sympathies to England.

As well, in New England towns, resentment toward Canadian Loyalists ebbed. The Federalist Party, popular in the northern states, valued the moderate virtues of the British model. This party was repeatedly defeated in the American Congress by the Democratic Party. In the eyes of the Loyalist elite, there were friends of England in the United States: These were the federalist elite of the northern states.

Throughout the nineteenth century, there were often annexationist politicians and journalists in the towns of the northern states. The annexationist ideal was espoused for different reasons: to increase commercial trade, weaken the power of the South, unify the Anglo-Saxon race. Some radical Irishmen (Fenians) even embraced this cause to get rid of the Crown on the North American continent, as a first step toward

e some prominent annexationists.
is-Joseph Papineau, who was des-
ic in the 1840s.

Liberal Louis-Antoine Dessaulles,
sur l'annexion du Canada aux États-
the red radicals opposed to cleri-
r Confederation; people such as
tte, and Honoré Beaugrand. The
iously and energetically defended
s living in regions connected to
ks (Montreal, the Richelieu Valley,

d a surprising number of annexa-
iberals in Montreal, Toronto, Hal-
d that annexation was a desired
nce of a commercial union (free
litics of John A. Macdonald upset
ry, as well as certain social classes.
nd artisans who had established
s dreamed of a full or partial re-
political barriers separating the

on of Canada and the Northern
rn under a name other than an-
f fusionism, insisting on the con-

What conditions would be necessary to give this movement strength? Five major conditions must combine, in a short
period of time, in order to crystallize fusionist forces.

First, a deterioration in the conflict that pits North against
South. Such an event is not inevitable. There could be a détente.
However, under the conflict scenario, southern Conservatives
would cause a national crisis, which threatens the union. Re-
publicans create chaos, which legitimizes their actions when
they choose to follow an imperial model. In so doing, they base
their actions on southern philosophy and alienate a growing
number of electors in the northern states. The Conservative
wing of the Republican Party, believing in an imminent catastrophe, throws caution to the wind in launching a crisis.

Second is the failure of the Quebec sovereignty movement.
As long as this movement represents a threat to federalist
forces, few politicians will want to think about other political
alternatives. If the proponents of sovereignty do not succeed
in obtaining a majority in the next referendum, it will lead to
deep reflection on this issue. Another defeat could mean the
demise of sovereignty. The Americanophiles could then find
sympathy for the fusionist ideal, in the sense that it would
guarantee political and cultural autonomy to its founding
states.

The third condition requires an aggravation of differences
in English Canada over the principles of the regime created in
1982. Indeed, Canadians are not unanimously satisfied with the
ideas contained in the Constitution. Most of the key elements
of the regime of 1982 (the Charter, multiculturalism, bilin-
gualism, equality of the provinces) are contentious issues in

the country's different regions. It is possible that the conflict between the pro-1982 and the anti-1982 factions could worsen and lead to the search for a new synthesis, one that could emerge from the fusionist movement. Accepting the failure of the patriation of the Constitution in 1982 would create fertile ground for the good reception of such a political path.

Fourth is the acceleration of the world energy crisis. The northern American states and the provinces of central Canada have similar economic and ecological points of view, halfway between economic liberalism and social democracy. Over the years they have learned to look for common solutions, and as such have created two entities: the Conference of Governors of New England and Premiers of Eastern Canada; and the Council of Great Lakes Governors. With regards to natural resources, these states are complementary. It could be that several northern states are more sympathetic to fusion, rather than a simple secession, in order to better benefit from Canadian energy resources.

The fifth depends on the action of the middle class of the northern states and central Canada. For a generation, these two groups have been weakened by the migration of economic activity toward the West and the South.

The economic elite in the northern states already is well aware of the economic consequences of the South's power in Washington. As for the economic elite in central Canada, this awareness is probably less advanced.

Economic power has certainly moved toward Calgary and Vancouver over the last generation. But until recently, political power was split over the Toronto-Ottawa-Montreal triangle.

The success of Stephen Harper's Conservatives will accelerate that reflection, for Canadian conservatism is now solidly entrenched in the West.

If such a movement started, it would likely unite first the eastern Canadian provinces and the New England states. Depending on the success of the enterprise, it could spread like wildfire.

Alberta would undoubtedly be the main Canadian province to resist the fusionist movement. On the American side, the Great Lakes states and the Pacific states could join the movement, because they belong to blue states (those that vote Democrat).

Many American states in these regions would be happy to see the foundation of a political community that marries the environment and the economy.

It would be difficult to precisely imagine the contours of such a political union. But it would undoubtedly be more secular, more social democratic, more pacifist, and more ecological than its southern neighbour.

The citizens of the northern states, as much as those in Canada, feel uncomfortable with the aristocratic regression that has affected the American nation for the last twenty-five years.

The growing wealth gap changed this society even more— a society once considered to be the cradle of modern democracy.

By abandoning its ideal of a middle-class democracy, the republic seems to be heading towards decline. This perception, shared by citizens of the northern states as well as those in Canada, will cause much anxiety in the future.

These sentiments could become strong enough to incite citizens on both sides of the border to reinvent democracy in North America.

This is not an ideal scenario, in my opinion.

But American upheaval, characterized by class struggles, a declining standard of living, and urban violence, could cause several regions in North America to choose the lesser evil in terms of solutions.

This sort of reaction would seek to preserve, whatever the cost, the thing that made this part of the continent great; that is to say a reasonable dose of social equality, economic prosperity, and political liberty.

CANADA'S ECONOMIC STRUCTURE: BACK TO THE FUTURE?

BY JIM STANFORD

IN THE 1860s, as the Canadian colonies were inching towards Confederation, British fire-and-brimstone preacher Charles Spurgeon exhorted the faithful with these words: "Find out your niche and fill it. If it be ever so little, if it is only to be a hewer of wood and a drawer of water, do something in the great battle for God and truth."

In economics, too, every country has a niche. And even as Spurgeon thundered from the podium, Canadians were struggling to define our niche in the global economy. Was it to be simply "a hewer of wood and a drawer of water," supplying raw materials to other more developed, countries? Or could the new nation aim for something greater in its economic future?

Resources have naturally played a central role in Canada's economic history. Our development has been largely shaped by successive resource booms: first furs, fish, timber, and agricultural goods, and later minerals and energy. These natural riches were harvested for export to our more advanced trading partners (first colonial Britain, then America). The resulting incomes paid for the importation of the more sophisticated manufactures needed on our farms and in our cities.

Analyzing this historical pattern, Harold Innis and other Canadian political economists worried that Canada's role as a hewer of wood and a drawer of water would constrict our prospects, leaving us perpetually dependent on wealthier metropolises to purchase and transform our resources, selling the more expensive value-added products back to us. So, from Confederation on, Canadian policy-makers became preoccupied with the need to expand value-added industries and diversify the national economy. Under the National Policy of 1879, tariffs on manufactured imports were increased to kick-start domestic manufacturing. Government invested heavily over the years in strategic sectors (from aircraft to telecommunications equipment), and used other policy tools (like made-in-Canada processing requirements) to leverage additional Canadian value-added. In 1965, the Canada-U.S. Auto Pact gave a particularly powerful boost to Canadian industry.

Gradually these efforts bore fruit, and Canada's economy began to escape from its traditional resource pigeonhole. One broad measure of this historical transformation is provided by the proportion of Canadian exports that consists of finished goods, rather than unprocessed or partially processed resources.

At the time of Confederation, Canada exported virtually no finished goods. By the end of the Second World War, 15 per cent of Canadian exports were finished products. The Auto Pact and other interventionist measures sparked further diversification, and by the 1970s one-third of our exports consisted of finished goods.

This proportion continued to grow in the 1980s and 1990s, as Canada's undervalued currency, relatively low labour costs, and growing technological capacities spurred investments in a range of high-tech industries.

By 1999, high-technology finished-goods industries (including machinery and equipment, automotive products, and other consumer goods) accounted for almost 60 per cent of Canada's total merchandise exports, and Canadian-made products (from cars to airplanes to personal telecommunications devices) were recognized around the world.

After 130 years of Confederation, Canada had mostly escaped its status as a resource supplier.

No one knew it at the time, but 1999 was a turning point, for Canada's economy quickly began to revert back to its former resource-dependent status. By 2007, barely 40 per cent of Canadian exports consisted of finished goods—down dramatically from 1999. The clear majority of our exports (surprise, surprise) once again consisted of unprocessed or partially processed resources: forestry, agriculture, minerals, and energy—especially energy.

Canada's energy exports have tripled since 1999. (Our exports of finished goods haven't grown a bit over the same time.) Canada is by far the largest source of imported oil for the United States—supplying more than Saudi Arabia, Iraq, and Kuwait put together. And considering all forms (including coal, gas, and electricity), Canada now produces more energy for the U.S. economy than we do for ourselves. Hence, Spurgeon's old adage should be slightly revised: Canada is now a hewer of wood and a pumper of oil.

But the structural turnaround in Canada's economy isn't solely due to the energy boom. Other factors help to explain this dramatic structural reversal, which is undoing many decades of deliberate and successful policy efforts:

The dot-com stock-market boom reached its peak in 1999. While many of the effects of that bubble were dubious and destructive, it did stimulate great amounts of research-and-development spending by Canadian high-tech firms, which created innovative products and successful exports. Since the bubble collapsed, R&D spending by Canadian businesses (always weak compared to other advanced economies) also collapsed.

By the late 1990s, China's dynamic economy began to make its presence felt in world trade. China's phenomenal growth has contributed to Canada's economic degeneration in two different ways. Our own finished-goods industries are being squeezed out of traditional markets (both at home and abroad) by low-cost, increasingly high-quality Chinese products. Meanwhile, China's growing hunger for raw materials has bid up global commodity prices (for now, anyway), reinforcing private incentives to allocate even more investment to resources.

In 1999, the World Trade Organization issued its first ruling against the Canada-U.S. Auto Pact, and the arrangement was eventually dismantled in 2001. This decision does not *solely* explain the historic downturn that has gripped Canada's auto sector since 1999. Most recently (and shockingly), Canada has become a net importer of automotive products—whereas in 1999 we were a top auto exporter. But the WTO has played a role. More importantly, it indicated that, under the new rules of globalization, interventionist efforts to stimulate higher-technology industries (as Canada always did, to try to escape its resource niche) are now harder (though not impossible) to implement.

Also beginning in 1999, Canada's dollar began to closely follow movements in international commodity prices. Initially this led to no great change. But by late 2002, as energy and other commodity prices began to surge, Canada's currency took off, and in late 2007 it reached par with the U.S. greenback. The loonie has thus increased over 60 per cent in five years—the fastest and highest currency appreciation in Canadian history. This has reinforced and accelerated the structural reversion of our whole economy: in a phenomenon known as "Dutch Disease" (which perhaps should be relabelled the "Canadian Condition"), a resource-driven exchange rate squeezes the life from manufacturing industries, which cannot survive such a dramatic deterioration in international competitiveness. And it's not just manufacturing at risk, either; every other non-resource tradeable industry (including tourism and tradeable services) has been hammered by this sudden 60 per cent deterioration in Canadian cost competitiveness. So far, unfortunately, federal government and Bank of Canada officials have judged this unprecedented appreciation as something to be celebrated (a sign of Canada's ability to "adjust to change"), rather than a problem to be managed.

More recently, Canada has experienced an incredible change in its foreign-investment relationship with the rest of the world. Among other developed economies, Canada was always uniquely dependent on foreign investment—although that stereotype, too, gradually withered away in the 1980s and 1990s. Indeed, by 1997, for the first time in our national history, Canada became a net creditor on foreign direct investment: Canadian companies owned more direct investment in other countries than foreign multinationals owned in Canada. The global commodity boom, however, has quickly changed all that. An unprecedented inflow of foreign investment and takeovers (worth $200 billion in 2006 and 2007 alone) has thrown Canada back into the "red" on our foreign investment account. On this score, once again we now owe more to the rest of the world than we own. This complements the historical regression in our industrial structure described above.

In the wake of all these developments, Canada is suddenly more reliant on natural resources than at any time in a generation. And in the absence of powerful countervailing policy measures to slow or counteract this trend, this pattern will continue in the years to come. Consider just one important resource export: petroleum. Canadian petroleum production is expected to double by 2020, to five million barrels per day (making us the fourth-largest producer in the world). This is entirely due to the expansion of production from Alberta's oil sands, which will make up 80 per cent of total output by 2020.

The technical and economic risks associated with mining and processing this sticky sand are now minimal. With oil prices exceeding US$100 per barrel (more than twice the break-even threshold for an oil sands plant), the oil sands have become virtually a licence to print money. Little wonder, then, that everyone wants in on the action: oil-sands development will attract $200 billion in new investment by 2020, dwarfing any other capital project in Canadian history. If prices stay at current levels, in 2020 oil will contribute well over $100 billion per year to Canada's balance of payments. Combined with huge inflows of foreign capital to oil-sands and other resource projects, this will ensure that our dollar stays high enough to seriously damage the whole range of non-resource exports.

A similar story, albeit less dramatic, can be told for other Canadian resource sectors. And of course, there are benefits as well as costs in this scenario. Jobs are created (especially in Alberta). Government revenues are generated (although the royalty regime for oil-sands plants, given their immense profitability and minimal risk, is scandalously lax). But an abundance of resources can be a curse, as well as a blessing, depending on how those resources are managed. And the economic, political, and environmental risks of placing so many eggs in the resource basket should give our policy-makers reason to pause, before they effectively endorse (through their inaction) this historic economic shift back to the future. Here are a few potential consequences to consider:

Well-paying jobs are created in booming resource industries—but not nearly as many as are lost in other export industries. Since the beginning of 2003 (when the loonie first took off), more than fifty thousand new jobs have opened up in energy and other resource sectors. That replaces less than one in seven of the four hundred thousand jobs lost in Canadian manufacturing over the same time.

The more significant employment shift spurred by the sky-high currency is from manufacturing into non-traded service industries: retail trade, hospitality services, and other sectors that produce solely for the domestic economy, and hence are mostly unaffected by the strong loonie. In 2000, exports accounted for 46 per cent of Canada's GDP. By 2007 that fell to less than 35 per cent (despite the energy boom). This is a strange process of "de-globalization": even as globalization marches on, Canada is curiously reducing its participation in global trade. Why? Because the overvalued currency and other structural factors make it impossible for anything other than resource industries to find a sustainable global niche.

An important consequence of this "de-globalization" is a slowdown in productivity. Domestic service industries are much less productive (in value-added per hour) than either manufacturing or resources. Putting more Canadians to work in those industries has thus significantly undermined Canada's productivity performance.

Resource prices are currently very high, as global commodity markets adjust to China's impact. But in the long term, real resource prices tend to decline due to technological improvements in extraction and processing. That trend will almost certainly reassert itself. If Canada's economy has become too dependent on resources in the interim, we will pay a big price.

Unfettered resource developments also impose significant environmental costs, both on Canadians and on the whole planet. In particular, the massive expansion of oil-sands production (which is itself a highly energy-intensive undertaking, long before the resulting petroleum is finally consumed) has been the most important factor behind Canada's miserable performance in reducing greenhouse gas emissions.

The uneven distribution of natural resources (especially energy) will cause major strains on Canadian federalism, in the absence of national-level efforts to manage and share the benefits of their development. Alberta's GDP per capita is now 70 per cent higher than in the rest of the country. Even more stunning, oil-producing Saskatchewan and Newfoundland are now the next-richest provinces according to GDP per capita. Indeed, these three oil-producing provinces are the only regions of Canada with GDP per capita higher than the national average; every other province (including Ontario and B.C.) is now considered a "have-not" province. Ironically, Canada is experiencing the most regionally unbalanced growth in its history, at the very time when the institutions of economic management and regional redistribution have been deliberately weakened.

MOST CANADIAN POLICY-MAKERS are not troubled by these longer-term risks and costs. They have accepted market signals (sky-high resource prices and profits) as authentic and efficient, and embrace the resulting restructuring of Canada's economy as reflecting some Spurgeon-like "natural" niche in the global economy. In contrast, I worry about the long-term economic, political, and environmental consequences of

Canada's re-emergence as a hewer of wood and pumper of oil. I think that Canada should strive for a broader, more sustainable, and more deliberate niche.

Canada needs focused efforts to more carefully manage resource developments, extract more domestic value-added from resource exploitation, sustain non-resource industries in the face of global trade and financial shifts, and share the benefits of resource development more broadly. Without those efforts, our national economy in 2020 will be precariously unbalanced, dangerously dependent on a handful of resource exports and the vagaries of global commodity markets.

I believe we could do a lot better with our vast resource inheritance. We could lever the wealth and opportunity represented by these resources to expand our repertoire of economic capacities, and nurture the skills and industries we will eventually need in a post-oil world. This will require proactive efforts to manage economic development, of the sort that have been out of fashion among market-oriented economists since the dawn of free trade twenty years ago. But in a long-term view, this interventionist approach would be quite consistent with the general thrust of economic policy through most of Canada's earlier economic history. Since we are presently heading back to a resource-dependent economic status, perhaps we should revisit some of the policy lessons from those earlier times, too.

A FORTUNATE COUNTRY

BY DAVID K. FOOT

IN 2020, annual economic growth in Canada is forecast to drop to an anemic 1 per cent. There is no recession. National economic growth has been declining for more than a decade. There is much hand-wringing among the nation's economic elite about this lacklustre economic performance, especially since economic growth in the United States is expected to be higher. But there should be no surprise. This difference in economic performance reflects, in large part, the higher fertility of Americans twenty years earlier, which has resulted in more consumers and workers.

Moreover, despite the continued claims from both business and government of widespread labour shortages, the unemployment rate in Canada remains mired above 5 per cent as older workers and immigrants continue to languish in the changing labour market. It appears that little has been learned from the previous twenty years.

That is not to say that government has been inactive. In the mid-2010s, Canada championed new legislation that, despite strong opposition from employers, outlawed ageism in the workplace and required employers to "respect and recognize" foreign credentials. It also required employers to pay for the skills upgrading necessary for new hires. This legislation imposed costly evaluation and retraining on employers. It also exposed them to potentially expensive lawsuits from immigration lawyers and well-educated boomers, now in their sixties and early seventies. Unrelenting demands for lower taxes and reductions in the size of the public sector left federal and provincial governments with insufficient resources to respond to these educational challenges, especially since health-care spending had absorbed all discretionary spending. The electorate was angry and had demanded action.

The quid pro quo for final passage of the legislation was a commitment to employers to raise immigration to levels that had not been experienced for a century. Nearly four hundred thousand immigrants arrived the previous year. Intake rules had been changed years earlier to permit limited numbers of unskilled and semi-skilled workers who were not immediately subject to minimum-wage laws, which caused much debate in the general population and especially in the immigrant community. However, employers were still "negotiating" with the various unions, professional associations, and government agencies over who would evaluate their credentials.

The debate created an unusual alliance, as both unions and professional associations united with employers in their opposition to the legislation. Yet it had become clear to many Canadians that employers wanted abundant cheap labour, while unions and professional associations were fighting to protect their incomes. No one appeared to be concerned about the increasing numbers of unemployed and the ever-widening disparities in income that had resulted from past policies. The public became increasingly disillusioned, so the new Egalitarian

Party used its balance of power in the federal legislature to get the legislation enacted.

Much of the debate had focused on declining standards of living and Canada's role in the global economy. Despite a decade of tepid economic performance and a divisive national debate, Canadians wondered why they were still admired globally. Faster economic growth in the U.S.—a Canadian benchmark—had not guaranteed American global domination or admiration. However, the Canadian economy had outperformed most other countries in the former developed world, including Europe, Japan, and other Asian nations. Canadians remained one of the better-educated populations, and natural resources, including open spaces, forests, diamonds, oil, gas, uranium, and especially water, continued to provide Canada with potential that many other nations lacked. Canada was viewed as a fortunate country.

In addition, continued Canadian workforce growth was envied in many countries now dealing with shrinking workforces. This moderate growth reflected somewhat higher Canadian fertility in previous decades and a long, well-established commitment to immigration. The economy continued to grow, albeit at a slower pace, and the Canadian quality of life remained high in global comparisons.

How could this be? Quality of life is difficult to measure. It depends on many things: the air we breathe, the leisure time we enjoy, the security of our persons and possessions, and, of course, our incomes. Choosing any one of these measures limits discussion, but understanding part of the picture contributes to an understanding of the whole. This is why economists often focus on an economic measure, namely income per person, which is sometimes referred to as the standard of living.

With slower economic growth, how could Canadians' standard of living be globally admired in 2020? A non-shrinking domestic population helped, as did continued participation in the expanding global economy. The incomes generated by selling at home and abroad the myriad of products and services produced in Canada added to incomes.

Also, it is important to remember that standards of living are measured in per-person terms, so the number of people that share in the income influences the outcome. For standards of living to rise, income growth must be faster than population growth. Alternatively, and perhaps of more relevance when populations decline, stagnant or even negative income growth can still result in rising standards of living, albeit for fewer people. Japan has become a prime example of this phenomenon in the twenty-first century.

Slower population growth became a reality for many countries of the world in the late twentieth century. By the early twenty-first century, population decline had set in for some, such as Russia and Japan. Not surprisingly, stagnant economic growth also became a reality. This did not automatically mean that these peoples were worse off. In fact, reducing the growth and especially the size of the human footprint had environmental benefits, thereby improving the quality of life as well as their standards of living.

The age of declining population growth and, in some countries, declining population size reduced the pressures for rapid economic growth. People came to understand that they could be better off with slower economic growth, even if business continued to pine for more rapid economic growth to sell their wares.

Why had economic growth slowed? Workforce growth was always the crucial determinant of a country's economic growth. The slower the workforce growth, the slower is potential economic growth. Whether the economy under- or overperforms relative to its potential depends on the share of the workforce that has jobs and the productivity of those who are employed. This depends on the behaviour of both employees and employers. High unemployment rates sap economic growth, while productivity performance depends not only on work effort but also on the quantity and quality of equipment provided to workers.

In many formerly developed countries, the baby boom generation had determined their economic history. In Canada, which had one of the "loudest" booms, the first boomer born in 1947 turned sixteen in 1963, while the last boomer born in 1966 turned sixteen in 1982. Consequently, Canadian workforce growth rose rapidly over the 1960s and, especially the 1970s, and then subsided in the 1980s. The impact of the birth control pill on births ensured slower workforce growth over the 1990s and into the new millennium.

Of course, not everyone enters the workforce at age sixteen. Increasing education reduced workforce participation in the younger adult ages and increased it in the middle working ages, especially for women. In the new millennium, workforce participation in the later working ages increased for both sexes.

This increasing workforce participation contributed to faster workforce growth. However, the inability of both the public and private sectors to enable the participation of aging boomers reduced the potential for growth. This lost opportunity contributed to worker dissatisfaction and, ultimately, slower economic growth.

Nonetheless, history had already set the scene for 2020. By the 1990s, workforce growth was one-third of that of the 1970s, so slower economic growth in Canada was well entrenched by the beginning of the twenty-first century. The fact that average economic growth over the 1990s was two-thirds of that of the 1970s implied that the country's workforce became more productive. However, overall population growth did not slow as fast as workforce growth, so the per-person standard of living did not rise as fast. Increasing productivity had not automatically produced increased standards of living, as many commentators had promised.

Recognition of the importance of population growth in determining workforce and economic growth led to receptivity in the general population for increased immigration, provided the immigrants were integrated into the workplace. However, despite rising immigration levels, population growth continued to slow. The entrenched below-replacement fertility levels continued to dominate.

More dramatic, however, was the slowing growth of the workforce. The first boomer had turned sixty-five in 2012, and while many boomers continued to seek work through their sixties, ageism and the pension inflexibilities frustrated their desires to keep working. Their search for flexible employment opportunities consistent with part-time retirement continued to meet resistance from employers.

This is what precipitated the demands for legislative solutions. By 2020, most of the first half of the boomer population had left the workforce. Average workforce growth over the 2010s was one-eighth of the growth rate of the 1970s! Slower economic growth mirrored workforce growth and fell to less than one-third of the economic growth rate of the 1960s. The alarm bells were ringing in the corridors of economic power, yet polling results showed Canadians happy with their standard of living. Why the inconsistency?

Slower economic growth certainly made management more challenging in the new millennium. There was less flexibility to reallocate resources in both the private and public sectors. In the more rapid-growth days of the past, management could reduce the relative importance of one area by freezing rather than reducing budgets elsewhere. That strategy became increasingly difficult when the pie was not growing as fast. As a result, pressure from shareholders and the press increased on management to be more accountable and more creative along the road to 2020.

Of course, any economic growth in excess of population growth increases the standard of living. However, as workforce growth dropped below population growth, this became more difficult to achieve. Attention became focused on the causes of continuing high unemployment and ongoing concerns about discrimination in the workplace, as well as boomer retirement and productivity performance. This attention sowed the seeds for the new legislation.

With increasing shares of new immigrants and older workers in the workforce, eliminating discrimination became an important part of the economic-growth challenge. For the immigrant workers it meant recognition of the skills that they brought from their homelands. For the older workers it became necessary to implement new policies to enable and encourage them to remain in the workforce. Policies that allowed workers to simultaneously add to and withdraw from pensions were discussed. But the reluctance of employers, unions, and professional associations to voluntarily confront the challenges led to the legislative initiative.

Nonetheless, as challenging as this scenario was for Canada, it was even more challenging for many other countries in the world. Canada had at least experienced workforce growth rather than the decline that occurred elsewhere. France, Germany, Italy, Japan, Korea, Scandinavia, and much of Eastern Europe (the Czech Republic, Hungary, Poland, and Slovakia) had faced declining workforces and many other countries, such as Belgium, Greece, the Netherlands, Norway, Portugal, Spain, and the United Kingdom had faced even slower workforce growth than Canada. This is a substantial list. Only Australia, the United States, and a number of smaller countries (Iceland, Ireland, Luxembourg, and New Zealand) had experienced faster workforce growth than Canada. And Canada had its natural resources. By comparison with these other developed countries, Canada had performed remarkably well in the twenty-first century.

Not surprisingly, this comparatively poor economic performance in the former developed world had led to a precipitous decline in its economic power in the global economy. There was no surprise in the increasing role played by the demographic superpowers of India and China, but China's need for international workers had taken the world by surprise. No pundit appeared to have anticipated the impact of the one-child policy on subsequent growth performance. New global superpowers were emerging from surprising places. Turkey in Europe, Brazil in South America, Vietnam in South Asia, and Iran in the Middle East were assuming leadership roles in their regions and in the global economy. The world was changing, and Canada was changing with it. Immigrants from these and similar countries were now business leaders in Canada and provided invaluable links that ensured Canada's continued presence in the global economy.

Slower workforce growth is inevitable in aging populations. The magnitude of the slowdown in many countries, including Canada, substantially reduced economic growth in the new millennium. This should not have been a surprise, or even a cause for concern. It is still possible to maintain continued rising standards of living if economic growth exceeds population growth. A number of countries were relying on shrinking populations to maintain their standards of living, but Canada was not in this group. With the gradual retirement of the boomers throughout the 2010s, immigration had played an ever-increasing role in population growth, and the controversial legislation had laid the foundation for bolstering workforce growth.

The road to 2020 had been largely predictable through the demographic lens. Canada had performed admirably, especially by comparison with most other countries in the former developed world. The good fortune of abundant natural resources had helped. By 2020, the country's standard of living and quality of life was universally admired. Historically "anemic" economic growth had become an asset, as had Canada's older workers and immigrants. And Canada's role in the global economy was as strong as ever, as it used its resources and immigrants to forge links with the emerging superpowers. Canada was indeed a fortunate country. And Canadians remained surprised!

CANADIAN FOREIGN POLICY IN 2020: A DIFFERENT PLAYER IN A DIFFERENT WORLD

BY MARIE BERNARD-MEUNIER

In 2020, Canada embarks upon a strong return to the international arena. Naysayers who predicted an inevitable decline in Canada's influence in the world are forced to eat their words. Indeed, Canada had spent a long time stagnating in a comfortable status quo, and it had experienced its own marginalization in a rather passive manner. The country believed that its dogged support of multilateral institutions, and its membership in all or most of the existing international organizations, would protect it forever and would secure it a spot in international affairs. But the world has changed.

The United Nations did not experience the golden age theoretically promised by the end of the Cold War. On the contrary, the Security Council was even more paralyzed than ever by the conflicting interests of the superpowers, and the whole system was suffering from chronic underfunding. The G8 had been replaced by a new group, the L20, which brought to the table all the main regional leaders. Even though it enjoyed a greater legitimacy, this group's impact was hardly any larger than that of its predecessor, but the main point was that Canada no longer had a place in the new group. Canada had long called itself a regional power, but the simple fact that it was not a leader of any region had finally caught up with it.

In Europe, NATO had been progressively marginalized. The United States had gradually lost interest in the "Old World," and the Europeans had decided to prioritize their own institutions. The European Union had finally managed to institute a common defence-and-security policy. Against all odds, the EU had managed to continue not only its growth, by integrating new members such as Turkey, but also its development, by the adoption of new common policies and by significantly growing the number of member-countries in the eurozone. The euro had actually gained equal status with the American dollar as a reserve fund and as a petroleum value instrument.

In Latin America, spearheaded by Brazil, the Organization of American States had also lost a lot of its importance. The Mercosur had become the touchstone for all of South America, including Mexico. In Asia, the Asia-Pacific Economic Cooperation (APEC) had died. The Association of Southeast Asian Nations (ASEAN) had doubled in membership, and Japan, China, and India had got together to convince all the countries in the region to establish a regional free-trade zone. The African nations had finally decided that nobody was interested in them, and they had stopped pretending that La Francophonie or the Commonwealth would do them any good.

As if by chance, everywhere in the world, institutions having member countries outside the region were losing their fight for survival. Some people interpreted this as a manifestation of anti-American sentiment, a product of George W. Bush's presidential mandate, but Canada was indirectly paying the price, because the institutions that were losing ground were the very ones to which it belonged.

Facing this rising tide of regionalism on all of the continents, Canada had naturally been forced to reflect on its own regional integration. For at least two hundred years, Canada had searched, a bit confusedly, for a point of perfect balance; that is to say for a way to remain close yet distanced from the United States. But now it was time to choose. It was finally necessary to decide, once and for all, yes or no, if our future would involve a closer relationship with the United States. In 2012, a strong majority government in Ottawa had asked for a mandate to negotiate an economic and monetary union with the United States, but a national referendum had overturned this proposal.

From one end of the country to the other, the debate raged. In spite of the spirited arguments of those who believed that an economic and monetary union was essential for the financial well-being of Canadians, political arguments had a much stronger impact. The "No" vote to economic and monetary union had won in the end (by only a slight margin in some regions) because the majority of Canadians were not convinced that such a union could mean anything more than pure and simple annexation of Canada by the United States.

The application of the free trade agreement had left many Canadians wondering about Canada's capacity to negotiate as an equal, or even to exert any kind of influence at all on the Americans. The refusal to respect Canadian sovereignty in the Arctic and the attempts to take over our water resources had simply been icing on the cake. It is true that the development of commerce with "emerged," rather than emerging countries had significantly reduced the importance of our trade with the U.S.

At the beginning of the twenty-first century, 85 per cent of Canadian exports ended up in the U.S., but twenty years later this had dropped to 60 per cent, and it continued to diminish.

Since the government had tied its fate to the outcome of the referendum, elections were held in the spring of 2013, and a coalition born of those factions saying "No" to economic and monetary union came to power. This coalition had promised to offer Canada new prospects for the future, especially with regard to foreign policy. In a Throne Speech dominated for the first time ever by this very theme, the government stated that, in order to regain its place internationally, Canada would have to succeed in accomplishing three things.

First, Canada would have to project a different image to the world, stronger and more independent, and this would not be possible unless Canada could manage to increase national unity and give its citizens a renewed sense of common destiny. This implied a renewal of the East-West axis upon which our country had been formed, but which had been neglected for too long in favour of the North-South axis. This also required that a long-term solution be found for the Quebec issue, notably an official recognition of the two founding nations; that a clearer and stronger role be established for all the provinces in the federation, as well as in the Senate; that an equitable compensation and recognition for aboriginal peoples be elaborated; and finally that multiculturalism be used as a means to consolidate, rather than tear apart, the fabric of our society. Indeed, this was an ambitious mandate that nobody expected would be easy to accomplish, but at least it outlined the challenge at hand and gave rise to a nascent new consensus for the country.

Second, in a world where each country had decided to give priority to its particular region, Canada had chosen to resist regional integration, and now it would need some strong new allies. Canada would need to transform its traditional relations, dictated by history and geography, into new, voluntary partnerships built with major players in all of the world's regions, especially in Europe and Asia. This would effectively allow us to consolidate our East-West axis by adding solid anchor points at each extremity, beyond Canadian frontiers and across the respective oceans. In so doing, Canada would be handicapped by its lack of experience. Historically, Canada had preferred multilateralism to bilateralism. Its only real bilateral relationship had been with the United States, and some would say, rightly so, that that relationship was based more on internal policy than on foreign policy. In the rest of the world, Canada had followed a policy based essentially on commercial interests, which is not wrong on the part of a large exporting country, but this sort of quest for new markets would not serve forever as a guise for foreign policy. Would Canada be able to manage to build multiple and varied alliances with a limited number of handpicked partners? The answer to that question would depend in large part on how Canada was able to manage its main assets.

This leads us to the third point. Canada would have to learn to strategically manage its main assets: its natural resources. It would have to learn to play "a winning hand." However, Canada had always been more comfortable playing the role of follower and peacekeeper. And there was no reason to be ashamed of this. The world would always need followers and peacekeepers, and Canada should remain ready to play these kinds of roles, but that in itself would not allow Canada to adequately defend and promote its own interests. In a universe lacking in raw materials, Canada was at least theoretically in a position of power. In order to translate that position of power into a real negotiating power on the international scene, Canada would be obliged first to rework its domestic policy.

The federal government would have to continue to support Canadian enterprises that had managed not only to survive but also to succeed in realizing the productivity levels needed to compete internationally. The government would also have to take all necessary steps to maximize the positive and minimize the negative effects of foreign investment in the natural resources sector. In so doing, it would have to avoid at all costs the temptation of stepping on provincial responsibilities and interests in this field. As for the provinces, they would have to show great wisdom in resource management, especially concerning aboriginal interests and environmental concerns. The provinces would also have to put aside the jealous defence of their responsibilities and rights in favour of contributing to the development of a national strategy for natural resources management and infrastructure.

In 2020, nothing that had been announced in the 2013 Throne Speech had been completely accomplished, but there was a new dynamic at work in Canada, and the country had succeeded in attracting the attention of the international community. The idea of regional integration had not died, but had been reborn in a different form. From now on, we would talk of an agreement involving Europe and North America. This idea of a transatlantic agreement was not a new one, but perhaps the conditions for its realization had finally come together. The rise of China had made the United States more modest and the European Union, having reached its limits and having even negotiated an agreement with Russia, was finally able to more clearly see the interests it shared with its neighbours across the Atlantic. However, public opinion in Canada was once again split between those who believed that this "occidental union" was exactly what we needed, because it finally gave us a larger arena in which to manage our unequal relationship with the United States, and those who were already used to the idea that Canada would continue along its chosen path: that of an assumed independence. The wisest among them, however, were well aware of the inevitability of integration into a larger entity.

BACK TO WORK: UNEMPLOYMENT AND THE FALL AND RISE OF CANADA'S TRADITIONAL VALUES

BY BRIAN LEE CROWLEY

THE CANADA OF 2020 is already foreshadowed by a thousand stories from 2008. Today, in Brandon, Manitoba, to keep their meat-packing plant operating at full capacity, Maple Leaf Foods has had to import workers from Mexico and Colombia, to whom the winters must seem a rude shock. In Prince Edward Island, there are dozens of Russian guest workers at a fish-processing plant, and a call centre recently left for want of workers. Despite the decline in manufacturing employment (a phenomenon shared with all mature industrialized countries), unemployment is still on a long-term decline, manufacturers are reporting growing shortages of skilled and unskilled workers, and wages are rising. Alberta saw its population rise by 3 per cent in 2006, and yet unemployment is still only 3.5 per cent.

Can this really be Canada, where not so many years ago a party won one of the biggest parliamentary majorities in history on the slogan of "Jobs, jobs, jobs"?

Yes, because that was then and this is now. When Brian Mulroney swept to power in 1984, it was more or less at the peak of the move of millions of baby boomers and women into the workforce. Year after year, barring recessions, a quarter of a million more people started looking for work.

The number of people of working age in the population rose from its long-term share of about 60 per cent in the mid-sixties to nearly 70 per cent today. A sustained increase of nearly 10 percentage points is an economy-shaking event, one about to be mirrored by a corresponding decline when the working-age population peaks in 2008 and labour supply starts to dry up in earnest in 2011–12.

Canadians did turn their minds to what to do with too many workers. Our answers have re-shaped Canada profoundly in the last forty years; we will spend the next forty years, to 2020 and beyond, undoing many of those changes, because the policies that emerged are the exact opposite of what is needed in an era of too few rather than too many workers.

The Boomer Revolution

The government liberalized unemployment insurance in the early seventies, overnight creating the "UIC ski team," a brilliant shorthand for paying people for most of the year in exchange for a token work effort. The real purchasing power of social welfare in much of the country rose significantly between the mid-sixties and the mid-eighties.

Many in those heady days benefited from programs such

as Opportunities for Youth, and Katimavik, which paid young people for being, well, young. There was a massive ramping up of our universities, warehousing for a few more years young people we scarcely knew what to do with.

Expectations of being able to retire early were pushed sky-high. Compulsory retirement became government policy, and buy-out packages a major topic of conversation in the company cafeteria. The Canada Pension Plan (CPP) gave the first generation of its beneficiaries pensions wildly disproportionate to the premiums they had paid.

We ran up an impressive national debt to pay for it all. But it wasn't just spending that got us in trouble; other things changed too. Immigration, for example, became less open, and we made it harder to bring in temporary workers.

Laws around the workplace changed. Trade unions and others saw an opportunity, at a time of anxiety about unemployment, to get gains for workers through political action. Minimum wages were driven up, labour-standards legislation gnawed away at employer prerogatives, protections against firing became more stringent.

In this same atmosphere barriers to trade between Canadians and with the outside world were raised through measures like the *Foreign Investment Review Act* and government requirements that broadcasters use a specific percentage of Canadian songs and programming on radio and TV. We eventually began to reverse course on protectionism with the Free Trade Agreement with the United States, but many barriers remain. In deference to the dairy farmers, who will brook no competition with butter, you still cannot sell yellow margarine in Quebec, even if it is manufactured elsewhere in Canada, and foreigners who have the temerity to try to sell us milk are charged tariffs of 270 per cent.

Public sector "employment" ballooned. Between 1960 and 1968, for example, the federal public service increased by over half and grew by a further 40 per cent over the next seven years. By 1977, StatsCan counted 330,000 federal employees, and another 144,000 in public enterprises. Transfers to the provinces shot up and had the desired effect, especially in low-growth provinces: today Ontario has 67 municipal and provincial employees per thousand residents, while Newfoundland has 99 and Manitoba 107. Much of this "pseudo-work" had little economic rationale but plenty of political payoff. CEO Paul Tellier was able to eliminate half the workforce of CN after privatization, because those workers were simply not needed to run a railway and had been there for political, not economic, reasons. Even today, as we teeter on the edge of a labour-supply cliff, burgeoning public-sector employment growth draws too many people from more productive pursuits.

One of the traditional motors of Canadian economic growth, labour mobility, was stalled by Employment Insurance (EI) and regional development policy until about 2003–04, when the huge wage advantage of working in places like Alberta started to outweigh the disincentives to moving we had created.

And in the face of all this policy designed to drive up employment and welfare dependence—whatever the cost in poor economic performance—Canadian policy-makers still professed themselves mystified by Canada's poor productivity relative to the United States. America had a boomer generation, but after some experimentation with big government in the sixties (remember the "Great Society"?), our neighbours largely returned to their traditional policy of reliance on the private sector and strong incentives for workers to get a job and get off welfare. The result for them? Between 1960 and 1998, U.S. per capita income grew by 222 per cent. The result for us? In Canada over the same period it grew by only 126 per cent.[1]

And despite the fall in interprovincial labour mobility, relative population shifts of great significance occurred, as those regions most reliant on the private sector soaked up workers and put them to work creating real economic value, attracted huge numbers of immigrants and had higher birth rates than regions mesmerized by the illusion that government-financed pseudo-work and welfare dependence were just as good as real productive work. By 2031, none of the StatsCan population projections show the combination of Ontario, British Columbia, and Alberta having anything less than two-thirds of the Canadian population, and that likely understates the political and population shift ahead. Their already waning appetite for financing unemployment-absorbing transfers will decline steeply when their economies start spluttering in earnest for lack of workers. Quebec, on the other hand, will soon have less than a fifth of the Canadian population, and will frighten the rest of the country less and less as its relatively declining standard of living makes separation an increasingly unpalatable proposition.

Out with the Old, in with the New

Worrying about unemployment is now *so* seventies and eighties. Today, newspaper accounts of labour shortages jostle on the page with stories about declining student numbers in the public schools. The boomers' legacy, however, is that we find ourselves still lumbered with a series of policies designed to mop up surplus labour at a time when we need to ferret out every worker we can find.

Today's falling unemployment is not merely some high in the economic cycle that will soon turn on us and drag us down again. We are entering a period of sustained and indeed growing labour shortages created mostly by bad policy, not market failure. We will find our growth constrained by our inability to find workers. Inflation will be an ever present danger in these tightening labour markets, as the Bank of Canada is already warning.[2] The standard of living of Canadians will be lower than it needs to be, just at the time we will need to find ways to pay for the retirement of all those boomers. According to the federal Department of Finance, by 2030 or so, population ageing will have caused Canadians to forgo economic growth of about 14 per cent of GDP annually compared to our current (unimpressive) growth path. To put that in practical terms, we will forgo about $25,000 per person in economic growth every year; a stunning loss of national wealth at a time when the claims of older Canadians, particularly on the health-care and retirement-security systems will increase.

The changes that are coming will not just be changes in this or that social program. We are about to undergo a values revolution or, more accurately, a return to many of the traditional values that underpinned Canada's great success in its first century.

For forty years or so, those traditional values—personal responsibility, a strong work ethic, an aversion to the corrosive effects that dependence has on individual character, and the centrality of family to civilized life—appeared to be on the wane. Our values adjusted to the bulge of workers by lowering our expectations of the contribution people should be expected to make to society. Traditional values appeared hard and uncaring in a world where real work was scarce, and the most socially vulnerable were the ones who fared the worst in the battle for jobs.

Shortly, however, it is the values of a social-democratic welfarism that will seem a quaint echo of a fast-receding past. By 2020, and probably well before, the political high ground will have been captured by those who understand how the anxieties of Canadians changed. Unemployment will be yesterday's issue, as the already anemic rise in our standard of living is further diminished by the fact that many jobs are going undone, new investments are being passed up, and profits are not being made, all because not enough people are available to work.

If voters relax their now-instinctive assumption that "there are no jobs," paying people not to work or to do pseudo-work will be transmuted from a social necessity that decent people understand and support to a costly extravagance that causes political resentment and friction. Because work will *be* widely available and will *be seen to be* widely available, welfare reform and elimination of pseudo-work will not be seen as an "attack on the poor" or a way of "blaming the victim," but as a way to confer on them the individual and social benefits of working. Public employment will be squeezed to free workers for more economically valuable roles and the provision of public services more reliant on good management and technology than armies of underemployed bureaucrats. Massive waves of retirement will help the transition. Welfare in its various guises will not be eliminated, but will shift from an *alternative* to working to an incentive *to* work. This has already been seen in embryonic form in the welfare reforms of the 1990s in Alberta and Ontario, provinces notable for having had the most robust private-sector job growth and therefore the least dependence on the public sector over the last forty years. More recently we have seen announcements of baby steps in this direction in more government-dependent provinces, including Quebec,[3] while federally we saw the introduction in 2007 of a Working Income Tax Benefit, or WITB, guaranteeing that even people at the bottom end of the income scale will be made better off by working than by staying on benefits.

Social inclusion, darling of the progressive left in the 1990s, will become the rallying cry of a new work-oriented social ethic. Aboriginals, some racial minorities, and some women are still not able to work as much as they may want to, nor up to their level of skill and ability. Decades of welfare for aboriginals and public-sector pseudo-work for all these groups has done too little to change their status. A labour shortage, combined with a government's determination to open the benefits of work to all who are capable of it, will make economic necessity the driver of real inclusion.

Those hoping for a quiet retirement will not escape these pressures. In an era of labour scarcity, "older workers" will be seen as a valuable resource to be kept in the workforce or enticed back. That is already happening: while we have had a poor record among industrialized countries in putting those over fifty-five to work, very recently the numbers of those continuing to work have started to rise more quickly than in other OECD countries. That rise will surely accelerate. Older workers will be pulled back into work by the increase in incentives that will reward work richly. And since remaining active and feeling needed by others are closely related to longevity and good health, this will change the retirement behaviour and political expectations of older Canadians out of all recognition. The relative balance of their concerns will shift to the tax burden, economic competitiveness, and flexible attitudes of employers and away from state-financed retirement benefits and social services.

Immigrants too will be high on the new work-driven agenda, as it will be imperative to make it easier to enter Canada, but the immigrants who come will need more support to integrate successfully, because they will bring fewer valuable skills, on balance, than in the past. Canadians had their pick of immigrants in the postwar world. No more. Now almost every country is actively pursuing the highest-value immigrants, and countries like China and India, now huge lands of opportunity, are trying to bring home much of their overseas diasporas, including from Canada. Immigration cannot even begin to compensate for the huge changes coming in the Canadian population. Newcomers would have to arrive in about seven times their current numbers if we wanted to stabilize the age structure of today's population. Such a rise seems hardly plausible.

A country with too few workers is also a country compelled to be open to trade; trade allows us to use other countries' workers to produce what we want. Provinces begging for workers will tear down the barriers to domestic trade. The new Trade Investment and Labour Mobility Agreement (TILMA) between B.C. and Alberta is only a precursor of a more liberal trade regime nationally. Free trade will be a touchstone of the new social and political order.

Reinventing work will become a social and economic imperative. This will include a re-examination of the old one-size-fits-all approach to labour legislation, workplace rules, and a host of other programs that will increasingly be shaped by the reality of labour shortages rather than the labour bubble of the postwar years. Working will be a more protean idea, and workers will have more choices and more power in the workplace than perhaps they have ever known. Parenthetically, that will make antediluvian trade unions even more irrelevant than they are today.

Put all this together: demographic reversal, massive increase in movement of Canadian populations, labour shortages, changing destinations of immigrants, accelerating decline of regions caught in the past, new political and economic power of growing and economically dynamic provinces such as Alberta, B.C., and Ontario (and, increasingly, Saskatchewan), a new congruence between traditional social values and the needs of the Canadian economy.

More work than workers will change everything. But the profoundest changes will not be economic; rather they will be social and cultural. By 2020, the resurgence of individualism, self-reliance, and devotion to work will be deeply entrenched. We will be well advanced into an era that will be as economically, culturally, and socially different from the last forty years as vinyl records are from MP3s and rotary phones are from BlackBerries. Yet ironically it will be an era that will be based on a resurgence of traditional values that the boomer era caused us to set aside. In 2020, we will wonder how we could ever have forgotten them.

Notes

1. Michel Kelly-Gagnon, "Big Government Impoverishes Us All," *Montreal Gazette*, February 3, 2001.
2. See for example the June 13, 2007, speech in St. John's, Newfoundland, by the then governor of the Bank of Canada, David Dodge.
3. Rhéal Séguin, "Quebec pledges nearly $1-billion to boost work force," *Globe and Mail*, March 19, 2008, A11.

CANADA AND ITS PEACEKEEPERS IN 2020

BY NOAH RICHLER

THE SWIFT AND UNPARALLELED rise to power of M., the Métis MP from New Brunswick who became, in 2018, the twenty-third prime minister of Canada, is generally attributed to the revelation, two years earlier, of the Calgary Tapes. Recorded in February 2016, by a member of the security firm hired for a petroleum company's party, the tapes show the assembled guests watching in silence as news footage of the Alberta bombings play on a television monitor overhead. Then G., the minister of defence, who as a professor emeritus of Canadian history was credited with having almost single-handedly de-bunked the country's peacekeeping myth, lets out a great whooping cry of *"Yeaaahhh!"*—a bray the likes of which had not been heard since Howard Dean's notorious scream at the Iowa Democratic convention of January 2004. G. turns, raises his glass, and shouts out, "I told you so! Didn't I tell you so? Now let those idiots stop us—it's about @&%king time!"

G.'s ugly display of relish at a terrorist attack on home soil, in which seventeen Canadians were injured and two died, constituted the turning point in the political fortunes of the Conservatives, who won a third consecutive election in 2014, and a majority for the first time—in what eventually became a twelve-year run—under the slogan "Security Abroad Begins at Home." The subordination, by then, of domestic issues to a foreign policy driven by the requirements of an unfettered and idealized military was a reality that had been driven home to Canadians the year before. Having won the election so emphatically in 2014, the Conservatives immediately made the mandate of the armed forces in Afghanistan an open-ended one—"Until the job is done," G. said. When, soon afterwards, the CBC used his pat phrase for the title of a sensationally popular radio comedy that reinvented the English novelist George MacDonald Fraser's cowardly hero, Flashman, as a Canadian officer in Kandahar (it quickly became a cult hit among NATO troops and the most downloaded series ever produced), G. drove legislation through that dismantled the national broadcaster, as well as the Canada Council, on the grounds that both institutions were "hotbeds of liberal lies supporting art without merit and the treasonous arguments of journalists incompatible with the necessary consensus and integrity of a nation at war."

Describing the petroleum company's party as "a private event beyond the party's jurisdiction," the prime minister—not for the first time—blamed "liberals and their sixties mentality" for dwelling on the Calgary Tapes "rather than on the bombings that caused the comparably insignificant incident." Having flatly refused M.'s demand for G.'s resignation, the prime minister promised, as usual, a "limited inquiry, rather than another flagrant misuse of taxpayers' money during hard times." He pointed out that only responsible Conservative fiscal management was preventing a full-blown economic crisis, though it was clear that his deflection was not working and the tide of popular support had begun to turn. When, after four months, whatever inquiry had taken place resulted only in the sacking of the security employee who had filmed G.'s cheers, M. rose from the Opposition's backbenches and asked—invoking, quite deliberately, U.S. Army attorney Joseph Welch's retort to Senator Joseph McCarthy—"Have you no sense of decency, sir?"

Having languished in relative obscurity until then, M. was suddenly vaulted to the front of the Liberal leadership contest, despite the fact that he was not officially in contention. M. was added to the party list not by his thirty-six sitting colleagues, but by rank-and-file members taking advantage of new cyber-rules introduced at the previous convention. Not yet thirty-two, M. won on the first ballot and quickly proved a capable populist. "Whoever loves Canada will not put in charge of our beloved country a man so evidently capable of invidious hatreds," said M. at the Prince's Park rally in August 2013, three days after the release of the Calgary Tapes and their wide dissemination on the Internet. Speaking to the more than one hundred thousand Calgarians in attendance, M. continued: "Whoever loves Canada knows that fighting for peace and not killing any prospect of it, is what we stand for."

It was G. who, that same year, had merged the Ministry of Public Safety with his own Ministry of Defence, and ruled in favour of the use of tasers and other weapons of "defensible force" not only by the RCMP but also by provincial police forces, ticketing officers, customs guards, transport and postal workers, utility employees, VIA Rail stewards, airline staff, electoral volunteers—and, "upon approval of the minister, any person likely to encounter unruly persons or deemed to be in a position of witness or fair suspicion of unrest or terrorist sedition." Now G. threatened to send the police in ("as peacemakers, if you get my meaning," he said) and accused M. of being a "blue-helmeted wuss who should not be trusted with the keys to the john, let alone the nation," a charge that swiftly backfired when it was revealed that, three years earlier, the new Liberal leader had been one of two Canadian peacekeepers operating in the Sudan. He had suffered several wounds, including one to the head, during the rescue of seven Bangladeshi peacekeeping colleagues from the Siege of Khartoum.

In Parliament, M. was eloquent. "Canadians defend with honour and, when it is required, with their lives, their ardent belief that only in the last resort should blood be drawn." Lifting the blue helmet that had been penetrated by a Chinese Kalashnikov round that narrowly missed his left eye, M. excoriated the government for its "allegiance to Mars, not Venus," and ridiculed its plans to build an armoury, costs to be paid by the developer of the attached condominium, on the erstwhile site of the Peacekeeper's Memorial (which had been removed to Grise Fiord, Nunavut, for "safe storage"). "No longer," said M., "will this nation tolerate the outrageous supposition that to be a supporter of peacekeeping is to be ignorant of our history, to be a coward, or to deny Canadian valour in some way."

M. continued in a fiery mood. "Let me tell you about our country. For well over a century, Canada has committed its soldiers in the service of the dominant power of the day. In the Boer War, that power was Britain's, as it was at Vimy Ridge, too. In the Second World War, Canadians fought for the Allied cause, and during the Cold War, and in Korea, we stood side by side with NATO and America, as we later did in Kosovo and then Afghanistan. Our service to UN missions—which we have allowed to be disparaged for over a decade now—is the historical extension of a commitment to a community greater than ours and of a peacekeeping nature that we have applied first of all at home. We proved it in Quebec in 1970, at Oka, Caledonia, and in numerous treaties since then. This is our heritage. Our peaceful commitment to a greater cause is the result of our history and our culture, and now it is time to return to it."

M. endured the subsequent ridicule of the Tory members in the House, who outnumbered the Grits by a staggering margin of six to one. However, for the first time there was in the Conservatives' hold on power a palpable undercurrent of nervousness. The ideas of the new leader—all of his comments, it seemed—were communicated with an enthusiasm not seen in years. They appeared on the Internet, but also on Global TV broadcasts and on the pages of the *Sun* group of newspapers, favoured media of the PMO, if only because their journalists and editors had grown bored of the government's dull news bites. And so, when G. announced, yet again, that recent polls only confirmed how grateful Afghans were to the Canadian Armed Forces for providing humanitarian aid and the security that made its delivery possible, M. had no problem taking his message of the army's "confusion of tasks" to the people.

In August 2016, the press watched as M. stood by the fenced military airstrip at CFB Trenton and waited for the caskets of the 379th and 380th Canadian casualties to come home. After two uniformed soldiers roughed M. up in full view of local police, the *Globe and Mail*'s embedded columnist dubbed him a provocateur, singing the praises of the military as usual. Nonetheless, M. was joined for the return of the 381st casualty by some five hundred protesters the very next morning. One of them, an army contractor, lifted M. in the bucket of his backhoe, from which he told the suddenly hushed crowd, "This is the story your government does not want you to contemplate. Your government does not want you to see that a soldier is human and dead in a war that is no longer about security, but about development and reconstruction, *which is a job for specialized peacekeeping forces and not combat troops*. The fact that Canadian soldiers are dying is tragic and I am in awe of their honour and their sacrifice but these men and women's deaths are not the *reason* we should stay. In Afghanistan, we have lost all good sense and purpose."

Over the ensuing months, M. refused to let the government off the hook for its unequivocal pro-military fervour and its augmented restrictions on the freedoms of the press and the people. He demanded a revocation of the amendments to the *Access to Information Act*, passed in 2012, and its "Improved Provisions for Release," which restricted the viewing of all government documents not approved by the PMO. He also pushed for an explanation of changes made to the *Tax Act* forbidding the claiming by artists of any expenses related to touring, travel, and public readings.

"Such frivolities are impermissible expenses in this wonderful age of podcasting and easy digital access," said R., the minister of tourism, sports, and national heritage. But the changes were widely regarded as an underhanded means of preventing demonstrations and the proliferation of anti-government sentiment, a sign of the government's dismay that the dismantling of the CBC after the broadcast of "Till the Job Is Done" had not sufficiently stifled criticism of the Conservatives.

When, in 2017, M. repeated his demand for an enquiry into the Calgary incident, by then a year old, it was actually the *National Post*, the last approved newspaper of the PMO, that leaked the Department of National Defence email to the minister ("We can't pay for everything all the time. Be happy. You have a nice house in Rosedale. What more do you want?") in which it was revealed that G., before his unelected appointment to the Senate and the Ministry of National Defence, had been paid in excess of half a million dollars annually through the Council for the Defence of Canada that he'd founded, for "work related to the promotion of military values in Canada." These funds had been expended on "research," which included, among other things, a small plane for weekend excursions to a newly acquired Georgian Bay cottage, holidays for his family, but also trips G. made with his twenty-nine-year-old "executive assistant" (a former Miss CFB Ontario) to Normandy, South Africa's Stellenbosch vineyards, Italy's Amalfi Coast, and various other "historically significant Canadian theatres of war."

"Who killed Canadian honesty?" M. asked, as again the prime minister promised he would get to the bottom of the scandal without abusing taxpayers' money. Which is when M., to the amusement even of several Conservative backbenchers bored at being ignored at caucus, praised the prime minister's evident thriftiness. "You have my vote," said M. "Canadians hardly need you to spend hundreds of thousands of dollars and a few years to establish what they have known since your predecessor took cash in brown envelopes and G. so fervently 'misspoke': your government is corrupt through and through."

When a video of M.'s performance was shown on the Liberal Party website, spreading to YouTube from there, the prime minister launched another lawsuit (his fourth in three years), a Conservative habit since the forgotten Cadman Affair seven years earlier.

But then M. did what his predecessors had never had the gumption to do—and laughed.

"You're a schoolyard bully," M. said, orchestrating, before the next day's sitting, thirty-seven separate statements of claim, one by each of his party's members, alleging libel by the prime minister and various of his staff.

"Our prime minister is an example of what Africans used to call the 'Big Man,'" M. told the YouTube network's Toronto correspondent. "He despises more than half of his constituency and believes that anything contrary that a person says is by nature traitorous and must be quashed. Here is a man who hates Canadian liberties. He's an embarrassment, and it's time we were rid of him."

In 2018, two full years after the release of the Calgary Tapes, the prime minister finally called an election, and M. said he would relish it. The ensuing campaign was fought, a third time, over the issue of Canada's participation in Afghanistan, but also over M.'s insistence on a "military plan for a country in which the promotion of peace is paramount and the extraordinary challenges of pursuing it not be shirked." M. argued for "an army for the new century, an army for a new world." His, he said, was a plan that would end the confusion of tasks on which the government had so cynically relied. It recognized Canadians' restored relationship with the Armed Forces, and the need for a continued investment in the military, but also addressed the problem of insufficient volunteers and the extraordinary array of complex tasks that now faced the common soldier. Under the terms of his plan for a "Blue Canada," M. proposed the creation of a military brigade dedicated explicitly to humanitarian work that, alongside the conventional Armed Forces, would provide "a true and workable expression of the character, will, and internationalist aspirations of the Canadian people."

Quickly, the Conservatives and a revivified G. heaped on the old criticisms. "What point is there in a further brigade doing a job the Armed Forces were doing already? Had M. not learned, in Darfur, that warriors are the best peacekeepers"— if, chortled G., there was anywhere "a peace to keep." M.'s "Utopian" thinking, said G., was "a masquerade for old-fashioned Canadian anti-Americanism and a boon for lily-livered liberal multiculturalists unaware of the dangers of war." To send Canadian soldiers into dangerous zones with light arms and restricted mandates was, said G., to make light of the ultimate sacrifice Canadian soldiers are called upon to make, recalling "the worst days of the country's hiding behind the shadow of Lester Pearson as a means of not adequately investing in our Armed Forces in the first place."

M. explained there was no reason to believe the arms would be light, but shortly afterwards, during the first debate, the prime minister accused M. of "not supporting our troops, of being patently against the guarding of our freedoms for which the army so valiantly stands."

"No," M. replied, "I support the army, but what I am against is confusion. Are Canada's Armed Forces in Afghanistan for reasons of national security—or, as your government has been pretending for several years now—for humanitarian reasons?"

"In Afghanistan we are in the process of building a nation," the prime minister replied.

"That's true," said M. "But the nation you are building is our own—and I've got news for you. It's already been built."

Support mounted for M. and his plan. One force, he explained, would be maintained for "national security," whether at home or abroad, and the other for "humanitarian" interventions, peacekeeping, and peace-building operations. A highly trained and well-equipped force, the latter would be deployed solely in the service of the UN, the African Union, and other peace-building alliances, according to the sovereign decisions of the Ministry of International Justice and Development that M. promised would be created by a new Liberal government.

M. said a new University of Peace Sciences would also be established, the successor, in spirit, to the Pearson Peacekeeping Centre that the Conservative government had replaced, in 2010, with a hockey school for new immigrants ("So they can learn what culture really means," said the minister of tourism, sports, and heritage, "and hopefully make good money and contribute to the tax base too."). The university would serve as a complement to Kingston's Royal Military College and make the essential point that peacemaking is an evolving craft, just as combat is.

"Now, in this fifteenth year of the war in Afghanistan," said M., "and in the long year that has passed since the Alberta bombings, it is incumbent upon us to find some better way forward—some way out of the terrible, age-old cycle of injury, retaliation, more injury, and more retaliation, that has been the pattern of all wars—until, finally, the players are exhausted and the possibility of peace finds its way into people's hearts again. Canadians cannot wait. We must, quite literally, jump the gun."

The new brigade, M. explained, would serve, "as the country has always done, the greater cause, but be comprised of exemplary citizens as well as soldiers, and be enabled to the highest degree. Our peacemakers shall be no less endowed than our conventional armed forces, but dedicated to the international community in the way envisioned by the original UN Charter of 1948. It will be a force that reflects and draws strength from our lawful, multicultural society, and it will be a force to which our young people can contribute much. Our peacekeeping force will be a part of Canada's template for a better world and make us a leader in it."

In time, said M., "Other nations will follow suit. In time we shall see that the last ten years constituted a Decade of Darkness in which not just soldiers but our politicians and journalists, and perhaps your neighbours, revelled in old-fashioned war fought by new means, as if conflict itself were something to celebrate—and not an appalling last resort. Let no one be ashamed to speak of 'Canadian Core Values' again. We know what they are and they are worth defending aggressively."

In November 2018, M. was elected to a majority in every province but Athabasca. In 2019, the RIM–Pearson University of Diplomacy and Development opened in Winnipeg, offering courses in engineering and reconstruction, languages and reconstruction, medicine and reconstruction, international law and reconstruction, et cetera. Chairs were granted to, among others, retired Generals Roméo Dallaire, Rick Hillier, and Lewis Mackenzie, physician Dr. James Orbinski, American author Samantha Power, American philanthropist George Soros, Professor Janice Gross Stein, and—the price of peace—G., who accepted an emeritus position in the Department of Reconstruction and Finance.

That same year, the First Canadian Peacemakers' Brigade was founded. The new "Blue Helmets" were quickly considered to be as expert in their international peacekeeping and policing realms of expertise as Joint Task Force 2 and the Devil's Brigade had been in theirs. The First Canadian was stationed at the refurbished Cornwallis Base outside Annapolis Royal and in Vancouver. In 2020, M. declined a UN entreaty to send the brigade to Sudan—the international community had waited too long to intervene, he said, the war was full-blown. But, as the Armed Forces continued their NATO-led policing of Helmand province in Afghanistan, the first mission of the new peacekeeping force started in Sri Lanka, where the performance of Canada's expert troops was bolstered by a substantial number of the bilingual officers of Tamil and Sinhalese descent.

SINCE TIME IMMEMORIAL
(PLUS TWELVE YEARS)

BY DREW HAYDEN TAYLOR

IF YOU ARE CHINESE, 2020 will be the Year of the Rat. If you are Native, it will probably be a year of concern, like a lot of years before it. The future is a very unsteady thing. It is a destination a long way off, as seen on a moonless and cloudy night, with only a vague and hazy memory of landmarks. For most of the trip, you use your hands to feel your way and your prayers to guide you. And the future is never what you expect; usually it's what you fear.

A thousand years ago, or more accurately in 1989, I wrote a play. It was the very first play I ever wrote and was lucky enough to have produced, a story about Native identity and options. It was called *Toronto at Dreamer's Rock* and it dealt with three sixteen-year-old aboriginal boys from different time periods. One was from four hundred years before, one was from the present (or 1989), and one, named Michael, was from the future, circa 2095. All were meeting together at the top of a sacred rock called Dreamer's Rock, which by the way really does exist, just off Manitoulin Island.

The image Michael paints of the future is not a pretty one. The aboriginal world he describes is unfortunately not that tragically different from the one with which we are familiar. In his time, he says, "We've lost our culture. It really isn't there. It's all been explained away or forgotten or just walked away from. Even our cheekbones are going. The poverty that once plagued us is gone but at what cost? The language only exists on digital disks, the sweat lodge is gone, and Dreamer's Rock is a tourist attraction." These are some of the issues currently being dealt with in almost every Native community in the country—though on some reserves the situation is more drastic than on others. At the time I was writing what I thought was a worst-case scenario out of a need to create dramatic effect; it was not meant as a prophetic vision.

I have always been a fan of science fiction and its possibilities, which is an odd admission coming from a Native person. It taught me that imagination and endeavour can create and anticipate practically anything. However, it's been my experience—rightly or wrongly—that First Nations people in general tend to view the world through the past. More than most cultures, they tend to view where they are now on the basis of where they used to be a decade or a century or five centuries ago. There are always discussions over what we've lost, what we are trying to get back, the way things used to be, and what would have happened if only the colonizers hadn't been so horrible to our ancestors. Land claims are about the past and how we ended up in the present. Language-immersion classes are about regaining what we are so close to losing because it was beaten out of our grandparents. Powwows are a celebration of culturally historic dances, food, and crafts, as filtered through a more commercial present.

For the aboriginal people of Canada, in many ways, the future has always been seen as something dangerous and to be feared. In science-fiction terms, we have been anticipating a dystopian future. In George Orwell's 1984, he envisioned a future where the government described the world that was to come, for a certain level of society, as "a boot in the face." About the time that book came out, Canada's Native people were facing residential schools, the beginning of the scoop-up/adoption fiasco, and a host of other programs introduced by a supposedly superior civilization that came from outer space—sorry, I mean Europe—in an effort to drag us out of the Stone Age and teach us the fine art of macramé and other dubious talents. I myself can heat and open a TV dinner. The whole situation reminds me of a plaque I saw on a store wall once. It said, "The only reason I hang around here anymore is to see what's going to happen next."

Overall, we as a people have not fared well as the march of years dragged us along, kicking and screaming. We drew and still continue to draw comfort and direction from the past. Each succeeding year has been responsible for more of who we were being lost, and the continued waning of indigenous fortunes. Unfortunately, the future was the enemy. At time of contact, it was estimated there were approximately a hundred million indigenous people in the Americas, mostly around Central America. Jump forward a hundred years, and they were down to about ten million, a 90 per cent decrease in one century. The future had brought smallpox and slavery.

That's just one example of how the future was whittling away at the aboriginal community. There are others. With every year that slips by, more of our languages are lost. In 1986, an analysis of the 1981 census data showed that, of the approximately sixty aboriginal languages that were spoken at time of contact, only Cree, Ojibway, and Inuktitut had a probability of surviving well into the next century. In fact, it showed that aboriginal people who listed an aboriginal language as their mother tongue in 1951 was 87.4 per cent, but in 1981 it was just 29.3 per cent. In just thirty years, one single generation, aboriginal linguistic fluency went down 58.1 per cent. Data from the 2001 census states that it is now only 13 per cent. The next census is in 2011. One can only guess what that will show.

Granted these numbers are statistics, and we all know how misleading they can be. There is an interesting statement I came across in, of all places, India, about the accuracy of statistics. Statistics are like a woman in a bikini (or man in a bathing suit, depending on your tastes); what it shows is very interesting; what it doesn't show is even more interesting. Many would argue that the explosion of the Native population in the last forty years, doubling, almost tripling, our numbers in that time, dilutes the negative impact of that 13 per cent. It's all how you read the map. In 1871, the Canadian census said there were a record low number of 102,358 indigenous people in Canada. In 2001, that number was up a bit: 1,172,790 Métis, Inuit, and First Nations people. Now that's a little more optimistic. The Vanishing Indian is no longer vanishing. Maybe there is hope in the future.

I know most of these statistics, other than our overall population, sound depressing and negative, but if there's one thing history has shown us, it's that history is seldom a laugh fest. It usually records more failures and tragedies than triumphs and reasons to celebrate. At least that's true in the Native community.

But there is one thing Native people have plenty of: hope. For the longest time, that's all they had. Hope for the future, hope for their grandchildren, hope for their people. And hope is the sole resident of the future, a one-way ticket of sorts. You tell anybody of an aboriginal persuasion out there that the culture they were born into and their grandparents passed on to them is disappearing forever, and, well, you've probably got a fight on your hands. We have survived what the future threw at us in the past, and for the first time in a long time, we actually have a say in what the future may offer.

Yes, in the 511 years since John Cabot (né Giovanni Coboto) landed on that far shore in Newfoundland, a lot around here has changed. But we acknowledge it's changed all over the world. Canada's Native people aren't the only ones being taken for an unfortunate ride through a radical future. Almost every indigenous culture, from the Sami in Northern Europe to the Maori in New Zealand to the Swahili in Africa have suffered in some way from the march of time. But, as the saying goes, that was then, this is now.

In some ways the dark cloud is lifting and the future seems a bit brighter. Most people are familiar with the famous saying by Louis Riel: "My people will go to sleep for one hundred years, and it will be the artists that awaken them." So, what are we waking up to?

What does the year 2020 hold? Well, Native people have to deal with the same issues white people have to. Issues like global warming. In my play *Toronto at Dreamer's Rock*, Michael tells of how things are in his time near Lake Huron: "That's when they purify the lake. It only lasts a week and then the water goes bad again. There's a new type of algae that thrives on ultraviolet rays and pollution. The lake is covered all summer long like a green blanket.... I envy the two of you. Being able to swim anywhere, even drink the water. It must be wonderful." When I was younger, water was your friend. Now, you can't be too sure unless it comes in a bottle. My grandparents wouldn't have known how to drink water out of a bottle. Paying good money for it would have made them laugh.

So, again, what does the future hold? Many of us have seen Chakotay on *Star Trek: Voyager*. Is that the face of our future, odd facial tattoos and a technological device that speeds up the vision-quest process? My, how we've progressed. Since very few of us are mystics or futurists or science-fiction writers, it makes it very hard to imagine where we will be as a people, though granted, the year 2020 isn't that far off. There is only so far to wander in twelve years. Look where we were in 1996.

An educated guess says we will no doubt be carrying on what we are doing now: dealing with political and social fallout from the last couple of centuries. Health and poverty issues will still be at the forefront of our efforts. People will be more concerned about the loss of the language and other cultural milestones. With global warming, the Inuit will be facing catastrophic climate changes that will affect their hunting, their very livelihood, not to mention the definite possibility of increasing water levels. Most of them live on the coast. Inuk refugee camps? Resource mining to feed the increasing need for oil and mineral ore will tear still more nations apart, as some want to preserve Turtle Island and others need to buy air conditioners to fight the increasingly high summer (and winter) temperatures?

When I started this essay, I had a much more optimistic view of what was possible because of my belief in the resiliency of our people. I am generally a very optimistic person. Being a humorist, I have to be. But it's the other people on this planet that have me concerned.

While we as First Nations were charged with the caretaking of the land (and, by association, the sea and air), we are not the people with the power to bring about that care. I don't know of any First Nations community with a coal-burning generating station or an oil freighter that has run aground somewhere, despoiling the environment. Unfortunately it seems as if we are unwanted passengers in a canoe that is racing for the rapids of worldwide climatic change. And since we are so tied to the land, I worry that what happens to it will happen to us. Creator knows we've had difficult times before, but this is a definitely a biggie. Resilience may not be enough.

All I know is that, in the year 2020, we will still be here. In 2040 or 2060, probably also. Though I don't know in what condition.

But I have my fingers and toes crossed.

CANADA IN 2020

BY AL AVLICINO,
CITIZEN ESSAY, PRIZE WINNER

THE 2010s was a challenging decade for the United States. The Chicago dirty bomb and the Miami and Houston hurricanes devastated three of her greatest cities, and her citizens had tired of the frustrating and fruitless entanglements in the Middle East.

President Hillary Clinton's administration saw her country revert to a 1930s-style isolationism to capitalize on the groundswell of support for continental integrity. It was a realization forced by the Sino-Japanese juggernaut that married Japan's technological savvy with a skilled workforce of nearly 1.5 billion, who would happily work a sixty-hour week for what their American counterparts earned in a single hour. So ferocious was their need for fossil fuels that the Asians began to outbid the U.S. for Saudi and Russian petroleum so that, even at $470 a barrel, there was none to be had.

The Continental Proposal was one that only a president in the last year of her second term could have made, and historians may argue that even she was surprised at the ease at which it was adopted. This made it much easier for President Barack Obama to spend his first term implementing the new structures. The American Union (AU) was clearly based on the EU model, but had learned from the Europeans' mistakes. The aspect of providing tiered membership with varying levels of autonomy was a master stroke, and proved to be the defining factor for its continental approval.

Massive approval of referenda established the new map of the North American continent. Quebec, Puerto Rico, Hawaii, Alaska, and the new state of Buffalo Commons (incorporating much of America's northern Mountain Time Zone) became the Outer Tier states, essentially independent republics that relied on the central government only for defence and economic harmonization. The rest of the U.S. became the Hub Tier, effectively a continuation of their previous status. The remaining Canadian provinces and territories became the Inner Tier, administered by their previous legislatures and co-existing in a Commonwealth Arrangement. Then there was the Special Tier, which consisted of a single area: Alberta. It maintained its autonomy as an Outer Tier state, but extended special privileges to any citizen who resided in the province as of January 1, 2016. These Albertans and their offspring had the right to cost-free, unlimited higher education, and benefited from the best health-care system in the world, a minimum guaranteed "middle-class" wage, and permanent exemption from all forms of taxes.

Under this system, Alberta almost overnight developed into the Dubai of the Americas, an enviable modern duchy with a staggering prosperity fuelled by its commitment to provide its enormous petroleum resources exclusively to the AU. This policy was responsible for the internal oil price stabilizing at one-third the world average, allowing the continental economic status quo to be maintained. Such unique energy affordability saw the size of the average AU house hold steady at approximately 2,000 square feet while the European equivalent shrunk to a claustrophobic 350 square feet. Citizens in the AU still drove their own cars long after the Europeans were forced to mass transit.

President Clinton's original proposals had included Mexico in an Outer Tier, but the unexpected election of a Mexican "Chavista" president forced President Obama to physically seal the southern border and had the southern Hub Tier states contribute over two million troops to enforce it. Obama also had to extend Hub Tier citizenship to all residents retroactively, which minimized the backlash from the Hispanic factions.

The implementation of the direct-democracy voting system from voters' home AmeriNet connection resulted in the November 2020 central election having an astounding "turnout" of 97.2 per cent. President Obama, running for the newly renamed American Union First Party, was handily re-elected to a second term by almost a hundred million votes.

Twelve years of what was once known as "Democratic Party" administration had allowed America to distance itself from its sometimes brutal role as the world's policeman. Isolationism paid benefits at every level of society, as the continent became self-sufficient in every economic aspect, from food to energy to consumer goods. The Inner Tier also benefited disproportionately, although not to the same degree as Alberta. The precious northern supply of fresh water was carefully administered by the legislatures now that global warming had made the southwestern Hub Tier desert states virtually uninhabitable and the Prairies suffered under their tenth straight year of drought.

On December 31, 2020, the eyes of the AU were on Point Pelee National Park, Ontario. While other New Year's Eves were traditionally celebrated with the ball dropping in Times Square, this one was marked by President Obama and Ontario Governor Ben Mulroney jointly planting a tree in the first banana plantation north of the Great Lakes.

A CANADIAN UNITY MANIFESTO

BY DAVE HAYWARD,
CITIZEN ESSAY, RUNNER UP

It began innocuously in the 1990s. An idealist penned a poetic manifesto, which, he felt, addressed Quebec-Canada unity issues. He periodically shared it with media, politicians, and leading personalities of the day. Notwithstanding the largely supportive feedback sent his way, it remained well out of the public eye. Often, he would not touch it for months.

But he could never forget it entirely. Certain highly disturbing incidents, widely disbursed over time and place and seemingly unrelated, propelled him into periods of deep thought and reflection. Progressively, a strong inner conviction took hold: his manifesto spoke to other domestic concerns, not just Quebec-Canada issues.

He concluded that the lack of a unifying national voice had somehow and in some way contributed to those disturbing incidents. They included: the one-man slaughter of fourteen female university students; the swarming and killing of a teenager by fellow teenagers; repeated Native protests and uprisings; a school-library fire-bombing; eighteen youths arrested on suspicions of terrorism; the mocking of citizens whose language, religion or appearance differed; the desecration of our cemeteries; and disrespect for our national monuments, symbols, and official languages. Added to these incidents was the discrimination and anger associated with unemployment and homelessness, drug and alcohol abuse, poverty, malaise, and despair—whether in our cities and towns, or on our Native reserves.

He wondered: Are these acts of anger, hate, and discrimination inescapable? Will our children and grandchildren witness the same? Have peace, acceptance, and hope become undeliverables?

Then he pondered his own past and realized that, in years prior, he had thoughtlessly wandered into the realm of anger and intolerance. His reflections quickened. What had influenced those missteps? Were they due to family beliefs and teachings, his community surroundings, his school environment? Had his thoughtless actions influenced others to think and do likewise?

Again, he considered his old manifesto. Like a wake-up call, he realized that, during his most recent years, he had become a decidedly calmer and more accepting person. He attributed this positive journey of change to the intimate influence of his very own Work.

Fast Forward to the Eve of 2020

Along with ringing in the New Year, forty-two million Canadians are discussing the nation's recent progress. They relish their accomplishments, especially the 2008 plebiscite, results of which our governments later consulted when drafting and signing a new Constitution.

For adults, that constitutional undertaking represented a new beginning. For youth, it foretold a future of enduring hope and opportunity for their generation and beyond. For all, it fuelled a period of listening and dialogue, understanding and reconciliation.

Focused and inspired, our learning institutions, governments, and NGOs responded by interpreting, applying, and teaching the constitution's underlying message, with special attention given to young audiences and new Canadians.

These initiatives won widespread approval, support, and community participation. Correspondingly, decades-old racial and language tensions, hate-based slogans and aggression, systemic discrimination, and schoolyard bullying and workplace harassment, all steadily declined.

Sick and poverty-stricken Canadians experienced newfound understanding and dignity, while the working poor discovered new opportunities and became more industrious and better paid, thus narrowing Canada's gap between the rich and the poor.

Duel strategies for the funding of safe drug-injection sites, in concert with enlightened prostitution legislation, contributed to safer streets and significant reductions in HIV/AIDS and hepatitis C infections. Issues surrounding Pride Day and same-sex marriage disappeared, while thousands more aboriginal youth undertook college and university training.

On other fronts, a major part of Canada's natural-resources revenue was being shared with resource-deficient constituencies.

That, combined with the elimination of interprovincial labour and trade barriers, saw the Canadian economy regularly outperforming powerhouses such as China and India. This opened the door for broad personal tax cuts and fresh government support for technology development in existing and emerging fields, such as telecommunications and transportation, health management, water and energy conservation, and the fight against global warming.

More recently, delegations from foreign countries arrived to visit and study our new Canada. From 2013 to 2018, three of these countries implemented their own constitutional changes, with each citing our Constitution as their model. Peace, health, prosperity, and good governance have since taken root: they are representative of Africa, the Americas, and Eastern Europe.

Shown below is that idealist's poetic manifesto from the 1990s, the essence of which was publicly weighed for inclusion in our Constitution's preamble. Following numerous and sometimes rancorous discussions, debates, and forums, country-wide approval was voiced by millions of Canadians in our 2008 plebiscite. Was your voice one of them?

We, the Descendants

We, the descendants of Canada's aboriginal, French, and English founders, and of all others who later arrived to help build this nation, stand in unity as witness to this pledge.

Remembering that Canada's provinces and territories have been settled by peoples whose mother tongues, heritage, and values differed, we pledge to one another:

A CANADIAN UNITY MANIFESTO

To recognize, to respect, and to celebrate Canada's diversity, lest a loss of identity suffers unto our descendants;

To embrace tolerance, equality, sharing, and compassion as the moral cornerstones of our great nation;

To bond together as one in the pursuit of dignity, health, prosperity, and happiness for all Canadians;

To forever preserve and promote this mission that we so proudly share.

PEACE, ORDER, AND GOOD GOVERNMENT: AN OPTIMIST'S OPUS

BY ERIC MANG,
CITIZEN ESSAY, RUNNER UP

WHEN PONDERING THE FUTURE, many of us conjure up fantastical sci-fi imagery. But as I sit here in 2008 and wonder what my country will be like in 2020, a short twelve years from now, the historian in me reflects on what life was like just over a decade and a half ago in 1992.

Let's have a very brief look at 1992: Brian Mulroney is a year away from resigning, the Tories a year away from almost ceasing to exist, and Jean Chrétien a mere twelve months away from being elected prime minister. Nunavut is on its way to becoming its own territory; Ralph Klein is elected premier of Alberta; Bob Rae is premier of Ontario; the Ottawa Senators are in the NHL; NAFTA is signed; a digital cellphone system is introduced in the U.S.; federal environment minister Jean Charest attends the Earth Summit in Rio de Janeiro; and we're listening to the Barenaked Ladies, Sarah McLachlan, and the Tragically Hip. I know people who are still driving 1992 Honda Accords.

History shows us that, for the most part, people aren't comfortable with rapid change.

Between 2008 and 2020, Canada will not suffer any terror-ist strikes. After briefly aligning ourselves with American foreign policy, we will rekindle our relationships with our kindred spir-its in Europe. Canada, returning to its original policies toward the Middle East, those being "fair minded and principled," will join other countries in a multilateral initiative to explore peace options with Hezbollah, Hamas, and al Qaeda. We will lead the world in promoting diplomatic solutions over armed re-sponses. We learn two things: Western meddling, such as in-vasions of sovereign countries, between 2001 and 2010, created more terrorists than it eliminated; and negotiations with terror-ists are possible and necessary, especially when those terrorists represent millions of people. Just as the IRA put its guns down, so will Hamas, Hezbollah, and al Qaeda.

Declining voter participation and the realization that mi-nority governments work better for all Canadians, leads us to adopt proportional representation. The Green Party joins the NDP and Liberals for what becomes known as the Stoplight Coalition. The sovereignist Bloc Québécois loses its relevance and ceases to exist. Taking its place is the newly formed Que-bec Unity Party, which seeks to strengthen Quebec's role in Confederation and pushes a platform demanding cultural and linguistic recognition. The QUP runs candidates in all 320 rid-ings and elects MPs in British Columbia, Manitoba, Ontario, Quebec, New Brunswick, and Nova Scotia.

The environment is a top election issue, as every party at-tempts to out-commit each other with their respective envi-ronmental platforms. The Tories, experiencing a renaissance after losing touch with voters, resurrect environmental policies from the Mulroney era and work with Green and QUP MPs to finally invest in the development of the hydrogen fuel cell as demand for oil wanes. All parties join together to block bulk water exports to the United States.

We become closer trading partners with India and China, but Canada also negotiates trade agreements with the South American Trading Bloc. A majority of Canada's trade continues with the United States, but is reduced compared to 2008. The U.S. has suffered due to years of heavy deficit spending and its unwieldy foreign-owned debt.

Vancouver, Toronto, and Montreal are busy, bustling cities. Investments in infrastructure and public transit, as well as changes in the workplace that allow for telecommuting, make these cities liveable.

New technologies reduce waiting lists and improve access to health care. Following an exhaustive review of studies proving that private health care is more expensive and guarantees worse health outcomes, federal and provincial governments accept the Rae-Romanow Report and re-invigorate and uphold the public health-care system.

Obesity is in decline because we eat better. Trans fats are banned, all food is organic, and every school offers an hour of physical activity every day.

We are a content society, building on and exploring the principles of peace, order, and good government. We're not an economic juggernaut, but we are celebrated for our values of social justice, tolerance, and fairness. The year 2020 will see Canada leading global peace initiatives, while reducing our environmental footprint and helping other nations do the same.

We will be a Canada that will find harmony between anglophones and francophones, and we will have started down the road to repairing the mistakes of our past with our aboriginal peoples. *The Simpsons* is still on TV, I'm driving my 2006 Honda Accord, and Sarah McLachlan's duet with her eighteen-year old daughter, India, is the hottest hit of 2020.

POSTSCRIPT

BY RUDYARD GRIFFITHS

WHAT SINGLE ISSUE or event could transform Canada by the year 2020? This was the question we put to twenty leading thinkers on July 1, 2006. Taken together, the essays this distinguished group wrote for the *Toronto Star* and *La Presse* paint the picture of a country bursting with potential, yet lacking the collective will to tackle a host of pressing future challenges.

Consider: the Earth's temperature rose half a degree Celsius over the course of the last 140 years—the period of industrialization in the West. If carbon-dioxide emissions continue to increase at current rates, experts predict global temperatures could rise by a full two degrees by 2020.

On the surface, a two-degree change in world temperatures hardly seems like a dire prediction. All we need to do is turn up the air conditioning a notch in the summer and then save a couple of bucks in the winter on heating costs.

The proponents of the "business-as-usual" approach to global warming forget that higher global temperatures increase polar melt. And with a hundred million people living within a metre of sea level—a one-centimetre rise in sea level translates into the loss one metre of flat coastal land—the impact of the projected twenty-centimetre rise in sea levels by 2020 could be catastrophic.

In other words, even using conservative predictions of the impact of global warming on sea levels, the world—and Canada—needs to prepare for a global migration, as hundreds of millions from the developing world are forced from homes and livelihoods into a desperate struggle for survival.

As a nation blessed with an abundance of habitable land, and a long tradition of humanitarianism, Canada will be expected to do its share to alleviate the suffering caused, in no small part, by our own carbon dioxide emissions.

Yet, here again, in terms of what the future could hold for Canada, we are vastly ill-equipped to deal with even current levels of immigration, let alone a deluge of environmental refugees fleeing the ravages of global warming.

Of the 250,000 immigrants who choose Canada each year as their new home, almost half eventually settle in Toronto. Project this trend to the year 2020 and a city that is barely coping with its current population of five million souls could have a total of eight million or more inhabitants. Thanks to the chronic underfunding of our settlement system, these three million-plus "new Canadians" will join the quarter of all immigrants who arrived since the 1990s and are living at or below the poverty level.

Canada is at real risk of creating a slew of failed "mega-cities" that lack the financial resources to deal with exploding populations of disaffected poor. Add to this hair-raising mix of interconnected forces the country's plunging birth rate, declining levels of civic engagement (e.g., voting), and growing regionalism, and Canada's future prospects could seem downright bleak.

But don't despair. On balance, our essays are hopeful about the future because of Canada's unique and privileged position in the world.

To start, Canada is protected by its geography from the worst of the political instability and violence in the world. We are also blessed with an abundance of natural resources that, responsibly managed, could fuel future economic prosperity. We also share many of the social institutions and values that saw previous generations through two world wars, the Depression, and countless political crises.

If there is one lesson I took from our Canada in 2020 project, it is that the future is, by its very nature, uncertain. We owe it to ourselves and the generation to come to press our present-day prosperity and security into service of a long-term vision for Canada to succeed in a changing world.

ABOUT THE
CONTRIBUTORS

Marie Bernard-Meunier holds a masters degree in political science from the University of Montreal and is a graduate of l'Ecole nationale d'Administration in Paris. She joined the Department of Foreign Affairs in 1972 and served as Canada's Ambassador to UNESCO, The Netherlands, and Germany. In Ottawa, she held various positions, including that of assistant deputy minister for global issues. Since retiring from the Foreign Service, she has been published in newspapers, public-policy magazines, and international journals. She currently serves on several boards, including that of the Public Policy Forum.

George Elliott Clarke, a native of Nova Scotia, has taught African-Canadian Literature at Duke University, McGill University, the University of British Columbia, and at the University of Toronto, where he is the E.J. Pratt Professor of Canadian Literature. Also a poet, opera librettist, and novelist, Clarke has earned a bevy of awards, including the Governor General's Award for Poetry (2001), the Dr. Martin Luther King, Jr., Achievement Award (2004), the Pierre Elliott Trudeau Fellowship Prize (2005), and the Dartmouth Book Award for Fiction (2006). His latest book is *Trudeau: Long March, Shining Path*, which has also been presented as an opera by D. Jackson.

Andrew Cohen is a professor of journalism and international affairs at Carleton University in Ottawa. He is a bestselling author and an award-winning journalist, who writes a weekly column for the *Ottawa Citizen* syndicated nationally in Can-West newspapers. Among his books are *While Canada Slept: How We Lost Our Place in the World*, which was a finalist for the Governor General's Literary Award, and *The Unfinished Canadian: The People We Are*. His latest book, *Extraordinary Canadians: Lester B. Pearson*, will appear in autumn 2008. In 2007–2008, he was a Visiting Fellow at the German Institute for International and Security Affairs in Berlin.

Brian Lee Crowley is the founding president of the Atlantic Institute for Market Studies, Atlantic Canada's public-policy think tank. He is a two-time winner of the Sir Antony Fisher Prize for excellence in think-tank publications, a former member of the editorial board of the *Globe and Mail*, a diplomat for the EU Commission, a negotiator of the Meech Lake and Charlottetown accords, a member of the Premier's Advisory Council on Health (the Mazankowski Committee) in Alberta, and a university professor teaching politics, economics, and philosophy. He has written many books, papers, and articles, including *The Road to Equity: Impolitic Essays*. Crowley was the 2006–2008 Clifford Clark Visiting Economist at the Department of Finance in Ottawa.

Don Drummond joined the federal Department of Finance upon completing his studies at Queen's University. During almost twenty-three years at Finance, he held a series of progressively more senior positions in the areas of economic analysis and forecasting, fiscal policy, and tax policy. Drummond joined the TD Bank in June 2000 as senior vice-president and chief economist.

David K. Foot, professor of economics at the University of Toronto, is co-author of the bestselling books *Boom, Bust, and Echo: How to Profit from the Coming Demographic Shift* and *Boom, Bust, and Echo: Profiting from the Demographic Shift in the 21ˢᵗ Century*. Foot is a two-time recipient of the University of Toronto undergraduate teaching award and a recipient of one of the nationwide 3M Awards for Teaching Excellence.

Pierre Fortin is an economics professor at the University of Quebec at Montreal. He has published widely in scholarly books and journals in Canada and abroad, mainly in the areas of economic fluctuations, growth, employment, and public policy. He has received many academic awards and distinctions, including a Governor General's Gold Medal and the Douglas Purvis Memorial Prize. He has been president of the Canadian Economics Association (CEA). He has also received the National Magazine Awards Foundation Gold Medal for his regular columns in the French-language magazine *L'actualité*.

Dr. Roger Gibbins is president and CEO of the Canada West Foundation, a public-policy research group based in Calgary. Prior to assuming the leadership of the foundation in 1998, he was a political science professor at the University of Calgary, where he started his academic career in 1973, and served as department head from 1987 to 1996. Gibbons has authored, co-authored, or edited twenty-one books and more than a hundred articles and book chapters, most dealing with western Canadian themes and issues. In 1998, he was elected as a Fellow of the Royal Society of Canada, and was the president of the Canadian Political Science Association from 1999 to 2000.

Chantal Hébert is a national-affairs writer with the *Toronto Star*, a guest columnist for *Le Devoir*, and a weekly participant on the political "At Issue" panel on the CBC's *The National*. She has served as correspondent for Radio-Canada as well as bureau chief for *Le Devoir* and *La Presse*, and is a Senior Fellow of Massey College at the University of Toronto. She is the 2005 recipient of the APEX Public Service Award, and in 2006 received the Hy Solomon Award for excellence in journalism and public policy as well as York University's Pinnacle Achievement Bryden Alumni Award. Hébert is the author of a 2007 book entitled *French Kiss: Stephen Harper's Blind Date with Quebec*.

Richard Hétu has been a New York correspondent for *La Presse* since 1994. For years he has been passionate about United States politics and history, writing about the shortcomings of American society through personalities like Michael Moore, Cindy Sheehan, and George W. Bush, among others. In 2002, he published *La route de l'Ouest* (VLB).

Stéphane Kelly teaches sociology at Cégep Saint-Jérome and political science at the University of Montreal. He has published two essays on the Canadian political tradition: *La Petite*

Loterie and *Les Fins du Canada selon Macdonald, Laurier, Mackenzie King et Trudeau.* He is also responsible for the scientific management and the French translation of *Canada's Founding Debates.* As well, he edited the collective work *Les idées mènent le Québec,* which traces the rise of a new generation of thinkers in Quebec.

Mark Kingwell is a philosophy professor at the University of Toronto and a contributing editor of *Harper's Magazine.* He is the author of twelve books of political and cultural theory, including the national bestsellers *Better Living, The World We Want,* and *Concrete Reveries.* He is a former columnist for *Adbusters,* the *National Post,* and the *Globe and Mail,* and the recipient of National Magazine Awards for essays and columns as well as the Spitz Prize for political theory.

Rachel A. Qitsualik is an elder of the Inuit culture, who grew up in the era of dogsleds and iglus (she avoided residential school, at the age of seven, by hiding behind a rock when the plane came to get her). She has a thirty-five-year background in translation and government work. In the 1990s, she made a jump to writing columns. By the twenty-first century, she had jumped to book writing, speculative fiction, and teaching. Qitsualik's writings are used as educational content in Canada, the United States, and Australia. She currently lives in Iqaluit, Nunavut, with her husband.

Noah Richler was raised in Montreal and London, England. He made documentaries and features for BBC Radio for fourteen years before returning to Canada in 1998 to join the *National Post*, where he was the first books editor and then a literary columnist. He has contributed to numerous other publications in Canada and the United Kingdom, including the *Globe and Mail*, *Maclean's*, the *Walrus*, *Granta*, the *Guardian*, the *Independent*, and the *Times*. His book, *This Is My Country, What's Yours? A Literary Atlas of Canada* was nominated for the 2006 Nereus Writer's Trust Non-Fiction Prize and won the 2007 B.C. Award for Canadian Non-Fiction, and his magazine writing has been nominated for National Magazine Awards. He was the host of the CBC's weekly review, *Richler on Radio*, and wrote and presented a ten-part series based on his research for his book for CBC Radio One's documentary program, *Ideas*. He is currently at work on a book about Digby Neck, Nova Scotia.

Jim Stanford is an economist with the Canadian Auto Workers, Canada's largest private-sector trade union. He received his Ph.D. in economics in 1995 from the New School for Social Research in New York, and also holds economics degrees from Cambridge University and the University of Calgary. He's the author of *Paper Boom* and of *Economics for Everyone*. In 2007, he was appointed vice-chair of the Ontario Manufacturing Council. Stanford writes a regular economics column for the *Globe and Mail*, and lives in Toronto with his partner and two daughters.

Daniel Stoffman's book, *Who Gets In: What's Wrong with Canada's Immigration Program and How to Fix It*, was runner-up for the Donner Prize for best book on Canadian public policy and the Shaughnessy Cohen Prize for best book on

Canadian politics. His previous work, *The Money Machine*, about the mutual-fund industry, was a finalist for the National Business Book Award. He is the co-author, with David Foot, of the bestselling *Boom Bust and Echo*, has written for most of Canada's major magazines, and has appeared as a guest on many television and radio programs. He holds a B.A. in political science from the University of British Columbia and a master's degree in international relations from the London School of Economics.

David Suzuki is host of the longest-running CBC series, *The Nature of Things*, which airs in more than forty nations. His 1985 series, *A Planet for the Taking*, averaged 1.8 million viewers per episode and earned him a United Nations Environment Program Medal (1988). He is the author of more than forty books, including, *The Sacred Balance*, *Wisdom of the Elders*, and *Good News for a Change*.

Drew Hayden Taylor is an award-winning playwright, novelist, columnist, and television writer. There have been over seventy productions of his plays in four countries, and he has published twenty books. Former artistic director of Native Earth Performing Arts in Toronto, he has dedicated his life to spreading the gospel of Native literature around the world. He is Anishinabe/Ojibway from Curve Lake First Nation.

Dr. David Walker is the dean of the Faculty of Health Sciences of Queen's University and chief executive officer of the Southeastern Ontario Academic Medical Organization

(SEAMO). He is also a professor in the Departments of Emergency Medicine and Family Medicine. Dr. Walker chaired the Ontario Expert Panel on SARS and Infectious Disease Control (2004), and the subsequent Expert Panel on the Legionnaires' Disease Outbreak in the City of Toronto (2005). He is chair of the board of the Ontario Agency for Health Protection and Promotion.

Jennifer Welsh is professor in international relations at the University of Oxford and a Fellow of Somerville College, and has taught international relations at the University of Toronto, McGill University, and the Central European University (Prague). She also spent five years in the private sector as a consultant, first with McKinsey & Company and then with Decode (a company dedicated to applying demographic research to private- and public-sector organizations). Welsh holds a B.A. in political science from the University of Saskatchewan and a master's and doctorate in international relations from the University of Oxford (where she studied as a Rhodes Scholar). She is the author, co-author, and editor of seven books and a series of articles on international relations. Among her most recent publications are *At Home in the World: Canada's Global Vision for the 21ˢᵗ Century*, and *The United Nations Security Council and War*, edited with Vaughan Lowe, Adam Roberts, and Dominik Zaum.